TORONTO WITH KIDS

The Complete Family Travel Guide to Attractions, Sites and Events in Toronto

ANNE HOLLOWAY

MACFARLANE WALTER & ROSS
TORONTO

Macfarlane Walter & Ross
37A Hazelton Avenue
Toronto, Canada M5R 2E3

Canadian Cataloguing in Publication Data

Holloway, Anne,
    Toronto with kids : the complete family travel
guide to attractions, sites and events

Includes bibliographical references and index.
ISBN 0–921912–84–6

1. Children – Travel – Ontario – Toronto – Guidebooks.
2. Family recreation – Ontario – Toronto – Guidebooks.
3. Toronto (Ont.) – Guidebooks. I. Title

FC3097.18.H65 1995   917.13′541044   C95–931404–0
F1059.5.T683H6 1995

The publisher gratefully acknowledges
the support of the Ontario Arts Council
and Webcom Limited's Unpublished Authors
Sweepstakes Programme

Printed and bound in Canada

For my two tireless researchers,

Adam and Curran

Acknowledgements

Unlike most authors, whose projects take them away from their families, I have had the good fortune of sharing my work on *Toronto with Kids* with my sons, Adam and Curran, and my husband, Andrew; their support and enthusiasm sustained me throughout. Thanks, guys.

From start to finish, Jan Walter of Macfarlane Walter & Ross showed graciousness, patience, and quiet tenacity. Sara Borins, Liba Berry, and Paul Woods adeptly assisted in ensuring the accuracy essential to a book of this kind.

I also want to thank Deborah Percy, for her able research on Toronto accommodations for families; Corinne Wyatt, for her valuable assistance with "Books About Toronto for Kids"; Barbara Czarnecki, who gave me the benefit of an expert final reading; and Diane Hargrave, who generously shared her marketing savvy.

I would not have been free to explore and to write about the best of Toronto for families without the indispendable assistance of Donna Beaumont, my kids' choice as Toronto's Best Childcare Provider.

And, of course, thanks to Toronto, the city that inspired it all.

Contents

Introduction

Until I had my own sons at a not very young age, and during the first hectic years of motherhood, I could not imagine an experience more draining or demanding than travelling with children. For me, travel was synonymous with freedom, spontaneity, and the thrill of the unfamiliar and the unexpected — all of the pleasures I had experienced on trips to Europe, the Caribbean, Sri Lanka, and cities across North America. My carefree image of travel certainly didn't jibe with what I feared were the dreary realities of dragging unwilling children through museums, force-feeding picky eaters in restaurants, and coping with kids who would rather be at home watching reruns of "Barney" or "Mighty Morphin Power Rangers."

Once Adam and Curran, now aged seven and five, got beyond the baby stage, I decided I had to face my phobias about travelling with children, or forgo what was for me one of life's most rewarding experiences. It seemed that the best, and cheapest, place to start was close to home: I resolved to look at Toronto, where I have lived for 34 years, as if I were a tourist — and to take the kids along for the ride. In recent years the boys and I, and their father, have visited countless Toronto sites, attractions, and events; wandered through a dozen neighbourhoods; strolled and hiked through a score of parks and ravines; eaten at lots of inexpensive, kid-friendly restaurants — and had the time of our lives along the way.

For the boys, the fun has been in going-doing-seeing, and they often request return visits to some of their favourite "discoveries," like the Metropolitan Toronto Police Museum, or Lambton Woods, or Wards Island. In return, their enthusiasm and fresh outlook have allowed me to experience, from a new and very special perspective, a city that is overwhelmingly rich in diversions and amenities for families. Enjoying Toronto's attractions in the company of youngsters is a treat that shouldn't be missed by either visitors to the city or its residents.

This pleasurable on-the-ground research led to the preparation and writing of *Toronto with Kids*. Unlike other guidebooks, *Toronto with Kids* focuses on how the city can be best explored and experienced by adults with children from infants to preteens. Its goal is to provide a helpful and entertaining guide to Toronto for visiting families and for locals, with much useful information to amuse, divert, and educate. I hope it will be the *vade mecum* of parents, grandparents, other relatives, care-givers, hosts to visiting kids — anyone, in short, seeking to entertain youngsters in Canada's largest and most diverse metropolis.

A guide of this kind can never be truly definitive, but every effort has been made to include up-to-date information on all of Toronto's major sites and kids' attractions and to anticipate the needs of the families who visit them. Boxed material and sidebars provide important information at a glance; a comprehensive index and helpful appendices lead readers to complete details on services and sites. Restaurant suggestions have been incorporated within the neighbourhood walking tours so that readers can combine sightseeing with noshing at kid-friendly spots along the way. (For further restaurant tips see the sidebar of other popular family eating spots on pages 186-7.) Similarly, shopping suggestions are listed in the walking tours and focus on stores that sell child-related products like toys, books, games, hobby materials, and clothing.

For most travelling families, being budget-conscious is the name of the game, and cost has been factored in as part of any recommendation. Prices are listed where available and are accurate at press time, but some changes are inevitable; regard all prices as an indication of the range of expense you are likely to incur.

I welcome suggestions for future editions of *Toronto with Kids* — recommendations, corrections, or criticisms. Kindly address them to Anne Holloway, c/o Macfarlane Walter & Ross, 37A Hazelton Avenue, Toronto, ON M5R 2E3.

Happy Toronto Touring!

Anne Holloway

April 1995

Greater Toronto Area

1 Black Creek Pioneer Village
2 Casa Loma
3 Exhibition Place
4 Fort York
5 Kortright Centre
6 McMichael Canadian Art Collection
7 Metropolitan Toronto Zoo
8 Ontario Place
9 Ontario Science Centre
10 Paramount Canada's Wonderland
11 Riverdale Farm

park areas

subway lines and stations

Downtown
Toronto

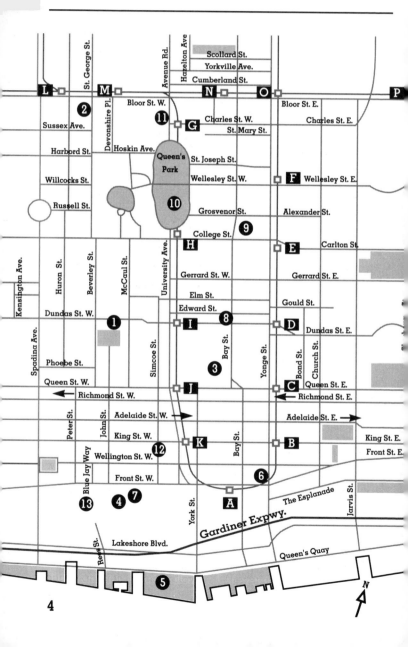

1 Art Gallery of Ontario
2 Bata Shoe Museum
3 City Hall
4 CN Tower
5 Harbourfront
6 Hockey Hall of Fame
7 Metro Convention Centre
8 Metropolitan Toronto Coach Terminal
9 Metropolitan Toronto Police Museum
10 Ontario Legislature
11 Royal Ontario Museum
12 Roy Thomson Hall
13 SkyDome

TTC Stations
A Union
B King
C Queen
D Dundas
E College
F Wellesley
G Museum
H Queen's Park
I St. Patrick
J Osgoode
K St. Andrew
L Spadina
M St. George
N Bay
O Bloor-Yonge
P Sherbourne

▨ park areas
–❑–❑– subway lines and stations

How to use Toronto with Kids

The one rule that should be followed by anyone touring with kids is **call first**. Nearly all of the listings in *Toronto with Kids* contain telephone numbers, and you can avoid the disappointment of a closed site or a cancelled event — or the shock of a too-high ticket price — by confirming the details in advance.

• The Greater Toronto Area (GTA) has two telephone area codes. The 416 code applies to all of downtown Toronto and those municipalities within Metropolitan Toronto; the 905 code is used for regions within the Toronto calling area. All telephone numbers listed in *Toronto with Kids* are 416 numbers, unless otherwise specified.

• Estimates of the length of time your family will need to visit an attraction (these appear under the **How long?** heading) generally allow for a quick lunch or snack break. These estimates, however, can only be approximate; your family's size, and the ages and interests of your children, will influence the amount of time spent at any given spot.

• Sites or attractions that best combine value for the money, originality, and family-oriented services and have proven their worth as consistent child-pleasers are awarded the teddy bear symbol ✱ of kid-satisfaction.

1: Ready, steady, go!

Toronto is a Huron Indian word meaning "place of meeting" and today the city certainly lives up to its name. Choosing Toronto as the destination for your family's trip puts you among the 28 million people who visit Canada's premier city every year — and don't worry, the kids will have lots of company: nearly seven million of these visitors are under the age of 17!

Why are so many smart travellers making Toronto one of the world's great sites for tourism? The answers are as varied and numerous as the advantages offered by the city. Like other world-class destinations, Toronto is exciting, vibrant, and cosmopolitan, but unlike some other cities in this class, it is also safe, clean, and efficient. How many cities operate an award-winning public transit system that one can ride in security day and night? How many host an average of 50 different theatre and dance productions every month? How many offer a beautiful lakeside setting, thousands of acres of wooded ravines, miles of wildlife-rich river valleys, and a vast island park where cars are forbidden and visitors are politely entreated to "Please Walk on the Grass"?

One American observer has called Toronto "a modern miracle — a city that has become better as it has become bigger," and with this growth has come a tantalizing array of sites and amenities that appeal to visiting families. One-of-a-kind attractions like the CN Tower (the world's tallest free-standing structure) and SkyDome (the world's only stadium with a fully retractable roof) lure visitors with their blockbuster status, but there are a great many other unique sites that make the city an irresistible place for all ages to explore. Imagine, for example, an intact 18th-century settlement nestled under the brow of an expressway (Todmorden Mills), or a 39-hectare (96-acre) lakeside entertainment and recreation complex that features family activities for all ages (Ontario Place), or a museum devoted exclusively to shoes (Bata Shoe Museum). These and Toronto's countless other attractions combine with some of the best shopping, dining, and cultural activities any North American city has to offer.

Toronto then and now

From its earliest days as a settlement, Toronto's well-protected harbour and its strategic location on a land route between Lake Ontario and Lake Huron have played

key roles in its history. The French used it as a fur-trading post until the conquering British made the town of York the capital of Upper Canada in 1793. York was a garrison town of 700 when, during the War of 1812, American soldiers burned down the government buildings and tried to seize the fort on the harbour.

During the 19th century, Toronto's (the city was so named in 1834) proximity to rich farmland, to a wealth of natural resources, and to major American markets, combined with the development of railways and the expansion of shipping on the Great Lakes, brought prosperity and allowed sober-minded and public-spirited officials to lay the groundwork for a modern city. A flurry of road construction, streetcar-track laying, and school, church, and hospital building created a lively, small metropolis out of what had been known as Muddy York just decades earlier, attracting waves of newcomers that swelled the population to 200,000 by 1899.

This steady growth in population, bolstered in the

20th century by the arrival of hundreds of thousands of immigrants from Europe, Asia, the West Indies, and Africa, has been a defining feature of Toronto's history, and today 3.2 million people call Metropolitan Toronto home. The city has become the financial, commercial, communications, transportation, and cultural capital of Canada, and a place where you can hear over 100 different languages spoken by over 70 different ethnic groups.

Getting ready

Before you and your family arrive in Canada's largest city, take some time to prepare for the trip. While perhaps not an art, travelling with children is certainly a skill, one that even the most apprehensive parent can learn. Planning is the key. Gone are the days of spontaneous side-trips and unstructured itineraries; serendipity has to take a back seat to preparation. Finding yourself in a strange city without a hotel room is an adventure when you are 20 and footloose; it's a recipe for disaster when you are 35 and cicerone for a couple of youngsters.

Planning begins the moment you choose your destination, and should involve the kids as much as possible, at a level appropriate to their ages. Children who have participated in some of the research and decision making are more likely to "buy into" the experience. For travellers considering Toronto, there are lots of books available that will acquaint young people with the city and fire up their enthusiasm for the trip. (A list of selected titles appears as Appendix 3.) Armed with a few of these titles, you can create a sense of adventure around the impending trip. What child wouldn't look forward to visiting a city that has a "real" castle (Casa Loma), or the country's largest amusement park (Paramount Canada's Wonderland), or the world's longest street (Yonge Street)?

An excellent all-round book on travelling with youngsters is *Trouble-free Travel with Children: Helpful Hints for Parents on the Go*, by Vicki Lansky. She makes the important point that travel itineraries work best if they are planned around the needs of

Short-stay itineraries

Deciding what to do and see during a stay in Toronto can be a challenging task when your family is confronted with a smorgasbord of choices. To help you out, the following short-stay itineraries offer combinations of sites and activities that are convenient, cost little, and have lots of variety for kids and adults alike. Note that some of the following attractions are not open year-round. Check the site listings for seasonal openings and hours.

2-day itineraries

DAY 1 Morning: Visit the Royal Ontario Museum.
Afternoon: Stroll through Yorkville to shop and gallery-hop, with time out in Yorkville Park. Late-afternoon tour of the CN Tower or SkyDome.
DAY 2 Morning: Enjoy Harbourfront; take a harbour boat cruise or Islands ferry to experience Metro from the water.
Afternoon: Visit the Ontario Science Centre (admission by donation Wednesdays after 4 pm).
DAY 1 Morning: Visit the Art Gallery of Ontario, then walk through Chinatown or the Queen Street West Village.
Afternoon: Enjoy the remainder of the day and early evening at Ontario Place.
DAY 2 Morning: Take the ferry to Centre Island; stroll through Centreville amusement park.
Afternoon: Visit the Hockey Hall of Fame — if your group has any leftover energy.

4-day itineraries

Follow the activities outlined for the first two days and add the following attractions.
DAY 3 Morning: Tour City Hall and the Eaton Centre or follow PATH through the underground walkway.
Afternoon: Walk through the Beaches neighbourhood and lakefront parks.
DAY 4: Visit the Metropolitan Toronto Zoo (full day).
DAY 3 Morning: See Casa Loma.
Afternoon: Stroll through Riverdale Farm or High Park.
DAY 4: Make a trip to the McMichael Collection of Canadian Art or Black Creek Pioneer Village or Paramount Canada's Wonderland (all full-day excursions).

the youngest child. While there has to be room for attractions and activities that will appeal to every member of the family, it's worthwhile to remember that a two-year-old will probably be happier in a playground than anywhere else. (With this in mind I have incorporated frequent mention of nearby parks in descriptions of Toronto's attractions.) Many younger children can't keep up with a full day of sightseeing, and the itineraries that appear on page 9 allow for lots of rest/play breaks and snack stops.

Before the day of departure, suggest to kids six and over that they keep a travel diary, beginning with their own list of the things they want to do and see in Toronto. While you're in the city, encourage them to pick up whatever "freebies" are there for the asking: matchbook covers, brochures, postcards, cocktail sticks. Later these can be assembled into a scrapbook, along with photos. A disposable 35-mm camera is an excellent investment: the kids can take their own snaps without your worrying about damage to expensive camera equipment. Don't

forget that older kids need a travel budget, spending money that they can ration according to their own judgement. Learning how to manage cash while they're away from home is an important lesson for your kids if you want them to grow up to be capable travellers later on.

Better safe than sorry

Certain essential precautions must be taken when you are travelling with children. Make sure to have all your family's health insurance information with you at all times, along with a list of telephone numbers of people to call in an emergency. (See Appendix 1 for Toronto emergency services.) Carry a detailed list of the medications your child takes, any allergies, or other medical data. If your child is taking a prescription drug, be sure to bring along a copy of the written prescription. You have only to imagine a situation in which you or your partner becomes injured or ill, and your children have to be entrusted to others even briefly, to realize that access to

How's the weather?

Cynics might say that Toronto has only two seasons: "It's not the heat, it's the humidity" and "It's not the cold, it's the damp." For travelling families, the important weather factors are that "spring" is often a misnomer in Toronto, where snow is not unknown in April, followed abruptly by summer-like temperatures in May. If you are travelling in these months, you'll need to pack a variety of clothing for everyone, and go for the layered approach on outings.

Winters can be harsh, but the odd balmy days do occur. From December through March, below-zero temperatures are the rule.

While snow falls may be frequent, all that clean white stuff is quickly transformed into wet grey slush by the heat of the city's buildings and cars; remember that waterproof boots and mitts are absolute necessities for the kids.

Toronto summers can be glorious if sticky, but most city natives would argue that fall is our best season, with still-warm days and crisp evenings. Because Toronto is an unusually "green" city, the changing colours of autumn are spectacular throughout the streets, parks, and ravines.

Constantly updated weather forecasts are available by calling 661-0123.

this information in a clear written form could be vital.

Of course, the even more frightening possibility of your child requiring medical attention during a trip must also be taken into account. I recommend that parents take out traveller's health insurance on *all* family members. The cost is outweighed by peace of mind, knowing that you won't be bankrupted by an away-from-home medical crisis.

One of the laws of parenthood is that if it can happen, it will, and most trips with kids seem to include a brief brush with minor illness, whether it's a cold, an ear infection, or tummy troubles. While a variety of remedies are

11

Great moments in Toronto history

1615: French *coureur de bois* Etienne Brûlé, in the company of Huron Indians, portages between Lakes Ontario and Huron; he is the first European to arrive in Toronto.

1750: The French construct a fortified post known as Fort Rouillé on the site of the present-day Canadian National Exhibition grounds. In 1759 the fort is burned by its French garrison as they flee from the British who conquer the territory.

1788: The British buy Toronto for £1700 ($9000) from the Mississauga Indians in a deal known as the Toronto Purchase. The purchased land block is 22 kilometres (14 miles) wide and runs 49 kilometres (28 miles) north from Lake Ontario.

1791: John Graves Simcoe becomes the first British lieutenant-governor of Upper Canada. In 1793 he names the Toronto site York; in 1794 he makes it capital of his settlement.

1812-14: York is twice raided and pillaged during the War of 1812 by American forces keen to control its strategic harbour.

1834: The rapid growth of York leads to its incorporation as the City of Toronto, with 9000 inhabitants and an elected civic government led by William Lyon Mackenzie as mayor.

1843: King's College, which evolves into the University of Toronto, first opens its doors to (male only) students.

1848: The city's first public school, donated by brewer Enoch Turner, is established.

1861: The first streetcar tracks are laid on Yonge Street to service horse-drawn trolleys.

1867: Toronto is made capital of the new province of Ontario at Confederation. During the following decade Toronto becomes industrialized and enjoys tremendous growth.

1875: Nurse Elizabeth McMaster founds the first Hospital for Sick Children in her home near the site of the present-day hospital.

1899: Toronto's new City Hall

(now known as Old City Hall) proclaims the civic pride of 200,000 residents.

1904: 8 hectares (20 acres) of downtown Toronto burn to the ground. A prohibition against wooden buildings leads to the distinctive brick construction of Toronto's architecture.

1905: The first Santa Claus parade has a handful of horse-drawn wagons and a Santa who arrives by train at Union Station.

1923: Foster Hewitt's first play-by-play broadcast of a Maple Leafs hockey game.

1951: Rapid population growth (1.2 million) leads to the formation of Metropolitan Toronto through the federation of the City of Toronto with 12 other, smaller local municipalities. Today Metro has six member cities — Toronto, Scarborough, Etobicoke, North York, East York, and York.

1956: Hurricane Hazel devastates large areas of the city, killing 81 and leaving thousands homeless. In the wake of serious flooding, construction is banned along the city's rivers. This leads to the creation of several of Toronto's most lovely ravine park systems.

1965: Staid Torontonians reel at the innovative design of their new City Hall, which quickly becomes Toronto's most recognizable symbol until the 1976 construction of the CN Tower.

1970s: A gradual shifting of financial and commercial activity from Montreal to Toronto and an overall economic boom leads to the construction of major new downtown banking towers and other skyscrapers that now mark the city's skyline.

1977: The Toronto Blue Jays play their first game at Exhibition Stadium; in 1989 they move to the newly constructed SkyDome.

1992 and 1993: The Toronto Blue Jays win the World Series Baseball Championship.

available in pharmacies, you can be almost certain you'll need one in the middle of the night. To eliminate a frantic search for the 24-hour drugstore in an unfamiliar city, consider including the following first-aid items when packing:

- bandages, sterile gauze pads, adhesive tape, disinfectant;
- infant and/or children's Tempra or Tylenol;
- thermometer;
- Pedialyte for dehydration;
- children's Gravol for nausea and motion sickness;
- cough medicine;
- sunscreen;
- medicated spray that reduces itching or pain from bites and scratches and soothes sunburn.

Pack up your troubles

Once you and yours are into the spirit of the trip, the next step is deciding what to bring. Again, those days of tossing a few items in a knapsack and hitting the road are long gone. Doubtless there are polar expeditions that pack more lightly than the average North American family on vacation, but anyone who has spent a

few hours in a car or on a plane with a bored child recognizes the necessity of having an endless array of amusements on hand. For my money, the two indispensable items are binoculars, which entertain kids of all ages, and a flashlight, if you are doing any night travelling.

Some babies obligingly sleep during the long hours spent in transit, but for those who don't you will need to pack a few simple toys. And remember, if you choose to bring something that squeaks or moos or plays a tune, you'd better be prepared to listen to it ad nauseam — and then some. Try to select toys that are more melodious, if you value your sanity. Tying toys to your baby's car seat will avoid those nerve-jangling screams that come when baby lets go of a toy and can't retrieve it.

For toddlers, fill up some old coffee cans or plastic ice cream tubs with small toys, like cars and action figures, including some they haven't seen before. (These containers may see double duty if motion sickness strikes.) Drawing tools like markers and crayons can be frustrating for very young travellers; they're always losing them under or behind the seats. Instead, consider investing in portable drawing toys like Etch-a-Sketch or MagnaDoodle.

For kids over four, drawing and colouring while in transit can while away many hours. Think about bringing along a clipboard or a cushioned lap desk to provide a hard surface for colouring books and drawing paper. Those activity pads that come with "magic pens" which reveal hidden designs are fun and easy to use on the road. Other useful items are felt-boards or Uniset reusable sticker sets (also great for sticking to car or plane windows), handheld puzzles and video games, a Walkman with tapes for private listening, and string for cat's cradle. While the $25 price is a bit steep, you might consider purchasing *Kids Travel: A Backseat Survival Guide* (Klutz Press). This book of puzzles, games, and other activities comes with its own clipboard and all sorts of neat stuff in an attached pencil case; it is always a

real hit with my young travel companions.

Many kids become carsick if they read while in motion, but picture books with little or no text seldom cause this problem. One brilliant idea recommended in *Trouble-free Travel with Children* is to staple together as many catalogue pages of toys as you can find; kids are born consumers and they'll pore over these contentedly for long and peaceful hours. If you don't mind doing a major clean-up of your car, then pack craft kits of coloured paper, scissors, glue-sticks, markers, stickers, and pastable odds and ends inside Ziploc bags and turn the back seat into a miniature artist's workshop.

In times of stress on the road, I have always resorted to the first principle of parental survival: feed them candy, fast food, pop...whatever flagrant exceptions to Canada's Food Guide will help restore harmony and equilibrium. Remember, it's a holiday for everyone, but it won't feel like one unless you're willing to relax your usual rules and routines.

2: Getting there and getting around

Visitors will have little trouble getting to Toronto: the city is at the hub of Canadian air, automobile, and train travel. Once arrived, they will discover a public transportation system that is efficient, safe, and affordable. And don't forget that Toronto is a great walker's city, blessed with a predictable grid street-pattern, clean public spaces, colourful neighbourhoods, and networks of ravine hiking trails.

Getting there

By air

Toronto is well serviced by several major North American airlines, by regional carriers, and by international airlines. When booking a flight, inquire about special fares; there are often considerable reductions for staying over certain days of the week or time periods. Airlines carry children under two for free if they ride in an adult's lap; if you want your child to sit in a safety car-seat for the flight, you will have to bring it yourself and pay the going rate for the child's passage. There are occasional discounts on children's fares, but these are limited depending on the number of seats filled by passengers paying full fare. Always ask about kids' fare reductions.

Airlines are happy to accommodate travellers with young children, offering pre-boarding services and seating behind the bulkhead, where there is more room. Parents travelling with infants under six months should request a skycot that can be installed

behind the bulkhead. Air Canada provides special kids' meals that feature popular fast-food items like chicken fingers and hamburgers, and the flight attendants also dispense such complimentary play items as puzzles, kids' magazines, and flight souvenirs.

A visit to the cockpit can be the highlight of air travel, an invitation that is extended at the discretion of the pilot. Just ask a flight attendant if you can go up and take a peek; it's a thrill for grown-ups too.

Lester B. Pearson International Airport

All three terminals of Lester B. Pearson International Airport offer a range of facilities to accommodate the travelling

family. Each has an **Info booth** and **Travellers Aid** desk on the Arrivals Level to assist you in accessing airport services. One feature that many airport users are unaware of is the nursery room to be found in each terminal. These locked facilities (doors are posted with

instructions on obtaining the key) offer diaper-changing tables, cribs, couches, even a few toys and books. First-aid services are available in each terminal free of charge from

17

6 am to midnight; go to the Info booth for assistance.

To travel between the terminals, catch the free shuttle bus that departs from the Arrivals Level every ten minutes, from 6 am to midnight, seven days a week. There is also an underground passenger corridor with moving sidewalks between Terminals 1 and 2.

Those long hours before delayed flights or between connections are even more stressful with young children. If you don't think that the numerous food outlets, shops, and video games rooms found in each terminal will be enough to sustain your family through the wait, consider renting a room at the **Sheraton Gateway Hotel**, which is attached to Terminal 3. The hotel offers a day rate of under $70 between 9 am and 5 pm. Guests are welcome to use the hotel's amenities, which include an indoor pool, a workout room, dry and wet saunas, and a Jacuzzi.

The airport also offers facilities for the disabled, including wheelchair accessibility and telephones for the deaf. Ask at any Arrivals Level Info booth for further assistance.

Lester B. Pearson International Airport
For information on the terminals' services call 8 am–11 pm daily:
Terminals 1 & 2: 247-7678
Terminal 3: 905-612-5100
Assistance available in English, French, and many other languages

Transit to and from the airport

Pacific Western Transportation runs frequent buses between Lester B. Pearson International Airport and three subway stations, and to all major downtown hotels. Service starts before 6 am and runs until 11 pm, seven days a week.

Fares to the downtown hotels are around $12 for adults or $20 return. The buses go to York Mills Station on the Yonge subway line; Yorkdale Station on the Spadina line; and Islington Station on the Bloor-Danforth line. Fares to the subway stations range from $7 to $9. Up to two children under eleven ride free on all buses; adult fare is charged for additional children. There are discounted fares for seniors. Buses run at

20- to 40-minute intervals and schedules are posted at pick-up points outside Arrivals Level exits. Your hotel reception staff will be able to give you the departure times, or call 905-564-6333 for information.

If you are staying at a hotel in the airport area, you may be able to take the hotel's complimentary shuttle from the airport. Use the courtesy phones on the Arrivals Level of any terminal to access these buses.

Taxis and limos to Toronto's downtown core are costly — approximately $35 for taxis and over $40 for limos, plus tax and tip. But if you have two or three kids, and everyone is tired and cranky from the trip, convenience may outweigh expense. Taxi and limo stands are found at the Arrivals Level exit of each terminal.

Drivers to the airport should be aware that the 7000 on-site parking spots fill up quickly and cost over $10 an hour. It's worth considering the

Travellers Aid

This charitable organization operates kiosks at Union Station and at all three terminals of Lester B. Pearson International Airport. Travellers Aid will find accommodations; offer assistance, including cash in some situations, to stranded travellers; give directions and help with transit connections; assist disabled or ill travellers; and attempt to provide information or services in a variety of languages. They will answer routine inquiries about events, sights, shopping, and so on, and they carry a selection of tourism brochures.

Travellers with children who find themselves in any kind of emergency — medical, financial, or social — should approach the Travellers Aid volunteers; they are trained to assist with every type of problem or to make the proper referral. All services are offered free of charge.

Union Station:
Open 9 am–9 pm daily, except Sundays
Room B23 on the
Arrivals Level 366-7788

Airport:
Open 9 am–10 pm daily
Terminals 1&3 : 905-676-2868
Terminal 2 : 905-676-2869

many off-airport parking facilities that provide shuttle service to the terminals; these park-'n'-fly lots charge around $10 per day or $40 per week.

Toronto City Centre Airport

Also frequently called by its former name, Toronto Island Airport, the City Centre Airport services commercial Air Ontario flights to and from Ottawa, Windsor, London (Ontario), and Montreal; it is also used annually by thousands of private planes. The airport is reached by a short ferry ride, which travellers catch at the foot of Bathurst Street. There is a parking lot at the ferry dock, or you can take the Harbourfront LRT from Union Station, get off at Spadina Avenue, and walk west to the dock. Another alternative is to ride the Bathurst streetcar to the end of the line at Lakeshore Boulevard, and walk down to the dock.

Toronto City Centre Airport is a great spot to watch planes do their stuff, and there are several observation areas at the terminal. If you ask the duty manager, he may allow the kids to stand on the balcony of the old control tower to witness the action up close. There is a restaurant at the terminal, but no other special facilities for families.

Toronto City Centre Airport

- For information on the terminal call the Duty Manager: 203-6942
- Air Ontario flight information: 925-2311
- Ferry: $3 for all passengers

By rail

VIA Canada's main passenger service, **VIA Rail**, runs numerous trains into Toronto's Union Station and offers connections to Amtrak and other American rail lines. Fares are discounted by 50 percent for children aged two to eleven; kids under two travel free. There are preboarding privileges for families with small children. Once settled on the train be sure to ask for the free VIA train cutouts and colouring books. Special services for children are minimal and there is no equivalent of viewing the airplane cockpit: the engine cabs are not open for visits. Newer cars have diaper-

changing tables in the washrooms and there are VCRs in the lounge of the Transcontinental, but the lounge is open only to passengers who have reserved sleeper accommodations.

VIA Rail Information
- Today's arrivals: 365-1220
- Reservations, schedules, fares: 366-8411, 6 am–10 pm daily

Visitors who travel by train have the advantage of arriving at Union Station, located in the heart of downtown and connected directly to the subway system. If your family finds itself with time to kill in Union Station, there is a pinball/video games room on the Arrivals Level. Travellers Aid (see page 19) operates a booth that is open daily from 9 am to 9 pm, except Sundays, and offers many kinds of assistance to city visitors. Union Station also connects with the underground walk-way that extends from Front Street to Dundas Street and to the Metropolitan Toronto Coach (bus) Terminal, which contains the shopping concourses that run under Toronto's major downtown skyscrapers. If you're in search of a place to get some walking exercise, grab a bite, or amuse the kids while waiting for a delayed train, head for the signs marked PATH (see page 173).

GO Transit

 The provincially operated **GO**

21

(Government of Ontario) **Transit** system operates trains and buses that service areas outside Metropolitan Toronto, to the east as far as Bowmanville, the west as far as Hamilton, and the north as far as Barrie, Guelph (northwest), and Uxbridge (northeast). Within

Toronto, GO connections can be made downtown at the Union Station subway stop and at various other points throughout the city. If you just want to take the kids for a

GO Transit
- GO Transit Information: 869-3200
- Train Service: Monday–Friday 6:45 am– 10 pm; Saturdays, Sundays, holidays 9:45 am–5 pm
- Fares: Charged by the distance travelled, special fares for children 5–12 years, kids under 5 travel free

train ride, then hop a GO train to a nearby destination. The fares are reasonable, the trains clean and comfortable, and there are some pleasing views of Lake Ontario if you head east.

By bus

Intercity buses all operate out of the **Metropolitan Toronto Coach Terminal** on Bay Street, just north of Dundas Street. Facilities at the terminal are meagre, but it is connected to the series of underground tunnels that run downtown to Union Station (see page 173).

If you find yourself delayed at the terminal, head across Bay Street to the two-storey shopping complex called the Atrium, with lots of restaurants and shops. The Eaton Centre is south of the Atrium, across Dundas; and west along Dundas Street a half-dozen blocks, you can take a stroll through the city's largest Chinatown.

Metropolitan Toronto Coach Terminal
General Information: 367-8747

By car

You shouldn't have difficulty reaching downtown Toronto from any of the major highways leading into the city, which are well posted with signs directing drivers into the core. Like most major urban centres, Toronto has fearsome rush hours from 7 to 10 am and 4 to 7 pm. Do whatever you can to avoid using the major arteries at these times, and be careful not to overstay your time at parking meters. The major streets are all posted with rush-hour parking restrictions that are aggressively enforced. Stay a few minutes beyond the allowable parking period and you are likely to find your car has been removed by a police-contracted towing firm. The cost of this small crime will be over $150 by the time you pay the parking ticket and an exorbitant towing fee.

You will be hard pressed to find inexpensive long-term parking downtown. Most lots have daily charges of over $10, and rates rise sharply from there. Fees of $3 per half-hour are common. Given Toronto's excellent public transit network, a car is usually unnecessary in the city core, so spare yourself the headaches and take the Toronto Transit Commission's "Better Way."

Getting around the city

 Public transit within Metropolitan Toronto is provided by the **Toronto Transit Commission** — the TTC — which operates subways, buses, and streetcars. This single-tier, one-fare system is highly reliable and easy to use, but try to avoid travelling in rush hours. Many visitors are impressed by the overall cleanliness of the subways, a point of pride among Torontonians.

There are two subway lines: the north-south route is called the Yonge-University-Spadina line; the east-west route is called the Bloor-Danforth line, and it intersects the Yonge line at Bloor, St. George, and

Spadina Stations. An additional RT line operates in the eastern suburb of Scarborough. Surface bus and streetcar routes all connect with a subway station and can be boarded for no additional fare. To be safe, whenever you board any TTC vehicle, you should request a transfer slip to ensure that you can make connections without additional payment. Transfers can be used on another route only during one continuous trip: you can't use them to make a stopover or to reboard the same route. If you are travelling only on the subway, and not on any surface routes, you can change lines and directions without restriction, as long as you don't exit the system at any point.

You will need a ticket, token, transfer, pass, or exact cash fare to board buses and streetcars. Surface-route drivers do not sell fares or make change. Tickets and tokens are sold at all subway stations and at authorized agents, most often convenience stores. Transfers are required between connecting routes; ask for them when you pay your fare.

The subway operates from 6 am (9 am on Sundays) to 1:30 am and trains are never more than a few minutes apart. So long as you are on the right line and heading in the right direction you needn't worry about taking the "wrong" train; all trains run a complete route at all times. If you are travelling at night, you may wish to use the platforms' Designated Waiting Areas (DWAs), which have benches, communications

Toronto's better way: the TTC

FARES

- **Adult:** Cash fare $2, 2-fare ticket $3, 5 tokens for $6.50, 10 for $13
- **Child (2–12 years):** Cash fare 50¢, 8 tickets for $2.50, children under 2 ride free
- **Seniors:** Cash fare $1, 10 tokens for $6.50
- **Day Pass:** $5 for one adult, good Monday–Saturday for unlimited travel after 9:30 am; on Sundays and holidays good for 2 adults and up to 4 children for unlimited travel all day

TTC INFORMATION

- **393-4636:** Information on fares, routing, and schedules, 7 am–10 pm daily; this number also accesses a multilingual service that offers information in 140 languages
- **393-8663:** Automated information service on major attraction routings, fares, subway hours, parking lots, and more; 24 hours daily; Touch-Tone telephone access only
- **TimeLine:** Every TTC surface stop is marked with its own unique TimeLine number, which will provide the times of the scheduled arrivals of the next three vehicles at that stop; 24 hours daily

- **Lost and Found:** Located at Bay Station, open Monday–Friday 8:30 am–5:30 pm; closed on public holidays; call 393-4100
- **Wheel-Trans:** For people with disabilities who can not use regular services; availability limited; call 393-4111
- **Washrooms:** Downtown in Yonge-Bloor and Eglinton Stations; also in Finch, Wilson, Kipling, Islington, Warden, and Kennedy Stations

features, and high-intensity lighting, all designed to enhance passenger safety. If you want to avoid being in an unattended subway car, travel in the front car, where the operator sits, or in the second-last car, marked with an exterior orange or white light, where the guard sits.

Kids of all ages love taking the subway, and given its convenience, it's the optimal choice for visitors moving around the city. Most major tourist sights are on the subway lines, and directions to these various destinations are often marked within the stations. If you have the chance, check out a couple of the stations that feature artwork commissioned

Trains and boats and planes

If modes of transportation thrill your kids, it's easy to entertain them in Toronto. As a Great Lakes port, a rail centre, and the country's major airline connection, Toronto offers ample opportunities to view the comings and goings of trains and boats and planes.

Trains

There are lots of choo-choos to be seen if you take up a post in the SkyWalk that leads from Union Station to SkyDome. As you look down, trains will rumble by right under your feet.

Boats

The eastern tip of Wards Island is a good place to spot large Great Lakes vessels passing through the Eastern Channel. If you drive down Cherry Street to the lake, you might just hit a time when the lift bridge is raised to let a boat go through the channel. The ferries to Toronto Islands (see page 93) offer the cheapest boat ride in the city and an opportunity to admire sailboats out on the lake.

Planes

There are two excellent locations to watch aircraft roar in and out of Lester B. Pearson International Airport. The most popular one, located just north of Renforth Drive on Silver Dart Drive, is a public access road that runs past the east end of runways 06R and 24L. This site has become such a well-known meeting place for aviation buffs that a hot dog vendor sets up his from some of the city's major artists. At College Station, adjacent to hockey shrine Maple Leaf Gardens, there's a mural of hockey players by Charles Pachter, famous for his "Queen on a Moose" series; at Queen Station, you'll find John Boyle's porcelain-enamel portraits of feminist Nellie McClung and Toronto's fire-brand first mayor, William Lyon Mackenzie.

At street level, don't miss a trip on a TTC streetcar. Toronto is one of the few North American cities that still operate these ecologically appealing vehicles, and since they ply many of downtown's main arteries, you won't have to find an excuse to ride one.

stand here during the summer. The other location is towards the north end of Lester B. Pearson at Airport and Orlando Roads. You won't be lonely at either of these sites, especially during the summer months when scores of plane aficionados enjoy the thrill of watching aircraft fly so close to the ground that it seems almost possible to touch them.

Although much smaller, the Toronto City Centre Airport, a short ferry ride from the foot of Bathurst Street, is one of the country's busiest airports with about 200,000 small-plane takeoffs and landings annually. To watch the action, go down to the airport ferry dock at the foot of Stadium Road or hang out in the great playground at Little Norway Park, which affords an excellent view of the airport.

Warplane enthusiasts should make sure they visit the Avro Lancaster Bomber, mounted on a plinth on the way into Ontario Place. Built in 1945, it operated as a search and rescue aircraft out of Newfoundland until 1964.

One annual event well worth attending is the Canadian International Air Show. Held every Labour Day weekend at the Canadian National Exhibition, this world-renowned show is a must for air enthusiasts of any age. There are breathtaking displays of aerobatics by both civilian and military pilots; in particular, the Canadian Snowbirds put on a fabulous show. Call 393-6061 for more information on the Air Show.

To pass a pleasant couple of hours, travel the entire east-west route on the Queen streetcar. You'll see some of the city's more interesting neighbourhoods: the Beaches in the east, trendy Queen Street West from University Avenue to beyond Bathurst Street, and the downtown shopping core, where you'll pass by old and new city halls and the Eaton Centre. Within the downtown core, streetcars also operate along King, Dundas, and College/Carlton Streets.

Families travelling on the TTC should be aware of the Day Pass. For $5 per adult from Monday to Saturday, and for groups of up to six people

(maximum two adults) on Sundays and holidays, travel is unlimited. If you plan to hop off and on the system throughout the day, this pass will save money and eliminate concern about whether you are making a "legal" transfer between two routes. Long-term visitors should inquire about a monthly Metropass (adults only) for unlimited travel.

For a complete overview and map of the TTC system, ask for a free Ride Guide at any subway station.

By taxi

Travelling by taxi in Toronto is not as sociologically fascinating as it can be in other cities. Metro cabbies are generally a fairly taciturn bunch, polite but not the chatty, ebullient types that we associate with New York or Chicago. A cab ride from Yonge and Bloor to Harbourfront will cost around $8, based on a fare structure, uniform to all the companies, of $2.20 plus $1.30 per kilometre. Cabs are usually plentiful on major streets or can be summoned by calling the major services: Diamond Taxi (368-6868), Yellow Cab (363-4141), or Beck Taxi (449-6911).

City tours

From April to November, **Greyhound Lines of Canada** (594-3310) operates two-hour conducted bus tours of the city that pass many major attrac-tions like SkyDome, the CN Tower, Harbourfront, and City Hall. You can board at the Coach Terminal at Bay and Dundas Streets or at one of several downtown hotels. Tickets can be purchased from the driver. Fares are $22 for adults, $16 for children eleven and under; kids under two ride free. During the off-season, bus tours are offered by **Toronto Tours** (869-1372). Both of these tours must be taken uninter-rupted; you cannot get off and reboard another bus later on.

A better deal, in terms of expense and convenience, is offered by **Olde Town Toronto Tours** (368-6877), which ferries passengers in a restored vintage trolley car and offers

commentary along the way. For fares of $21.95 for adults and $9.95 for kids up to twelve (kids under five ride free), you enjoy a two-hour ride with the option of getting off and on as many times as desired, as long as you don't try to reverse your direction. Tickets may be purchased from the company's kiosk in the basement of the Royal York Hotel, at Bay and Front Streets.

During the tourist season (May to October), several companies operate boat tours of Toronto Harbour and Toronto Islands that are always popular with kids. **Mariposa Cruise Line** (203-0178) ferries up to 200 passengers in a replica-Victorian steamship for a one-hour guided tour; **Toronto Tours** (869-1372) has three boats running on a frequent schedule. Call the tour operators for departure times and fares, which are in the range of $14 for adults and $8 for children (kids under two ride free).

Where to find out what's on

Toronto has many sources that offer information on the city's family attractions and events including:

City Parent

A free monthly newspaper tabloid with an events calendar, attractions listings, a column on dining out with kids, and features on child-raising issues. Available in libraries, bookstores, toy stores, and other children's retailers. Call 905-815-0045.

eye weekly

A free entertainment tabloid with reviews and event listings. Available in restaurants, bookstores, theatres, and some retailers. Call 971-7186.

NOW Magazine

A left-leaning alternative weekly entertainment tabloid, with reviews and event listings. Available free in restaurants, bookstores, theatres, and some retailers. Call 461-0871.

Talking Yellow Pages

A free 24-hour telephone service. Call 283-1010 for general information; press 3010 for an events listing, and 3130 for a "What's On for Kids" listing. Touch-Tone telephone access only.

Today's Parent

A monthly national maga-

Specialty tours

Aside from city tours, there are a number of specialized tours that operate chiefly in the summer months. The information here is current as of publication, but arrangements can change. Telephone to confirm times and other details.

All of the tours listed below welcome families, but you should consider the age-appropriateness of the tour and whether it meshes with your children's interests. Most tours are best suited to youngsters over eight, or are great for families with babies and toddlers in strollers (especially if they sleep). If you call ahead and notify the tour guide that you will be bringing along children, he or she may be able to adapt the commentary to engage young participants.

Toronto Historical Board Tours
Every Sunday from May 1

zine that publishes a special insert for the Toronto market nine times a year. Available at news-stands and by subscription; the insert is distributed for free to some bookstores, libraries, and children's retailers.
Call 598-8680.

Toronto Life
A monthly magazine with feature articles on Toronto people, places, and goings-on. Monthly event listings include a "Child's Play" section. The July issue contains the Kidsummer calendar (see page 153). Available at news-stands and by subscription. Call 364-3333.

Toronto Star
The Thursday "What's On" section of this daily newspaper contains weekly entertainment and event listings. Available at news-stands, corner boxes, and by subscription.
Call 367-2000.

Where Magazine
A free monthly magazine published in cooperation with the Metropolitan Toronto Convention & Visitors Association. Contains articles, restaurant listings, and events calendar. Distributed in hotels or available by subscription.
Call 364-3333.

through September, the Toronto Historical Board offers free guided walking tours that explore different aspects of the city's past: everything from Toronto's military to its theatrical history. Most tours begin at 1:30 pm but points of departure vary. Call 392-6827.

Toronto Field Naturalists' Club Tours

This volunteer organization, dedicated to the study and preservation of the city's natural heritage, runs various free tours throughout the year which introduce participants to Toronto's many urban wilderness areas. Some of the tours are quite long and specialized, and may be unsuitable for families. All tours start near an access point of public transportation. Call 968-6255.

University of Toronto Campus Tours

Free tours of one of North America's oldest and largest universities are offered in June, July, and August. Student guides conduct hour-long walks through a campus that has often played Harvard or

Princeton in the movies. Picturesque 19th-century buildings are highlighted and if you're lucky, the famous Ghost of University College might put in an appearance. Tours run weekdays at 10:30 am, 1 pm, and 2 pm and are available in English, French, Portuguese, and Hindi. Call 978-5000.

ROMWalks

Twice a week, from the beginning of June right through September, the Royal Ontario Museum offers 13 different guided walking tours that convene at starting points in downtown or midtown Toronto. Most of the one- to two-hour walks are free. Sunday walks start at 2 pm; Wednesday walks start at 6 pm. Call 586-5513.

Underground City Tour

Toronto's vast underground city runs from Front Street up to Dundas Street, with numerous offshoots along the way. For the uninitiated this terrain can feel like a frustrating maze. To take the mystery out of the subterranean network, enjoy a guided walking tour that visits North America's only underground golf course. Meet outside the Sheraton Centre Toronto Hotel, opposite City Hall. Tours run weekdays in the summer at 9:30 am and 1:30 pm. $10 for adults; discounts for children. Call 905-486-9111.

Ghostwalks

The only guided tours of haunted Toronto, Ghostwalks offer an entertaining and eerie perspective on many of the city's historic buildings. Discover the lunatic ghosts of Queen's Park, the poltergeists of Old City Hall, and the restless spirit of a murdered stonemason at the University of Toronto. Ghostwalks are two hours long and run June through September; Tuesday to Friday at 1 pm and 7 pm and weekends at 3 pm. $10 for adults; $6 for children under 12. Departures from the corner of Bloor Street and Queen's Park. Call 690-2825.

Chinatown Walking Tour

This walk includes visits to a Chinese herbalist, a tea shop with hundreds of teas, and an artist's studio, and a cooking demonstration by the tour leader, restaurateur and chef David Ko. Though it's an expensive undertaking for a family,

the tour does include a large Chinese lunch and pickup from downtown hotels. Over three hours in length, tours start at 9:30 am daily, year-round. $48 per person; possible discounts for children who are not eating a full meal. Call 599-6855.

Toronto Architecture Tours

Tours of Toronto's financial district that concentrate on both historic and contemporary architecture. Daily at 10 am except Tuesdays; 3 pm on weekends. Meet on the steps of Old City Hall. $10 for adults; discounts for children. Call 922-7606.

Outdoor Art Tours

Toronto has a wealth of outdoor art, including murals, sculpture, and mixed-media installations. These tours start at Union Station's outdoor clock. They take in SkyDome, with Michael Snow's unique sports-fan gargoyles, and circle back west, ending up at the Sculpture Garden at King and Church Streets. Tours run June through Labour Day, at 10 am and 2 pm daily. $10 for adults, $5 for children ages 10–16; children under 10 free. Call 537-3627.

3: Now I lay me down to sleep

Toronto's accommodations are as varied as the city. You can choose from cozy bed and breakfast homes, apartment hotels, college residences, and budget, mid-priced, and luxury hotels. There are hotels that overlook wooded ravines, Lake Ontario, or the playing field at SkyDome. You can stay right in the thick of downtown or on the city's fringes, near attractions like the Metropolitan Toronto Zoo.

The accommodations highlighted here have been chosen according to several criteria: location, availability of kitchen facilities, special family rates, programming and amenities, and access to recreational facilities are among the features families look for. The rates quoted are for double rooms; surcharges for children are indicated. All rates are subject to change at any time, so be sure to confirm rates when you make your reservation.

Families' needs and budgets will differ; the following information is intended to help you locate the accommodation that offers the services your family requires. Those marked with a ✱ offer outstanding amenities within their category.

The following three organizations book room reservations within Metropolitan Toronto free of charge. These services save the trouble of phoning around and sometimes offer rates that are cheaper than those you would be quoted if you called yourself.

- **Accommodation Toronto**
  905-629-3800

This is a centralized reservation service operated by the Metropolitan Toronto Hotel Association. Offers booking for hotel rooms only.

- **Econo-Lodging Services**
  494-0541

This service, run by a group of the city's apartment hotels, is for visitors wanting short-term furnished apartments, which are often ideal for families.

- **Toronto Visitor**
  Information Line
  1-800-363-1990

This number, which services North America, puts you in contact with the Metropolitan Toronto Convention & Visitors Association. Assistance is offered with accommodations and many other aspects of your stay in Toronto. Touch-Tone telephone access only.

Apartment hotels

My family became enthusiastic converts to apartment hotels during a recent trip to Ottawa. The convenience of having a full kitchen and a washer/dryer along with a roomy one-bedroom suite was unbeatable. Because our kids define the term "picky eater," we loved being able to prepare our own meals rather than negotiating restaurant offerings three times a day. In the mornings, it was a relief to laze around in our pyjamas and enjoy a familiar breakfast, without having to pay inflated hotel prices or rush down to the restaurant before it stopped serving. While they may have fewer services than large hotels, for most budget-conscious travelling families, and especially for those planning stays longer than a few days, apartment hotels are ideal.

Glen Grove Suites ✱

2837 Yonge Street
Toronto ON M4N 2J6
Tel 489-8441 1-800-565-3024
Fax 440-3065

- Midtown residential neighbourhood location on the Yonge subway line, 15 minutes from downtown
- 63 suites $65–$90, children under 18 free
- Parking included
- Suites include full kitchens with stoves and microwaves; VCRs, and colour TVs; movies and video games for rent at front desk
- Cribs and high chairs available
- Babysitting available
- Non-smoking floors
- Pets allowed

- Coin-op laundry
- No restaurant but tuck-shop on premises
- "Mini" health club, sauna, and exercise room

- Guests may use facilities of the Sport Club of Canada at Yonge Street and Eglinton Avenue ($10 charge per day); childcare centre and children's programs offered at the club for an additional charge

Bay Bloor Executive Suites ✱

1101 Bay Street
Toronto ON M5S 2W8
Tel 968-3878 1-800-263-2811
Fax 968-7385

Close to Bloor-Yorkville and the Royal Ontario Museum

- 123 suites $79–$149, children under 18 free
- Weekend packages available
- Parking $7.49 per day
- Suites include full-size kitchens, microwaves,

stove and fridge, cable TV with pay-per-view movies; Nintendo games for rent

- Cribs available
- Disabled access
- Babysitting available
- No non-smoking floors
- Pets allowed
- Coin-op laundry
- No restaurant but guests are given menus of nearby eateries that will deliver to hotel
- Indoor heated pool, sundeck and sauna, exercise room

Alexandra Apartment Hotel

77 Ryerson Avenue
Toronto ON M5T 2V4
Tel 504-2121 1-800-567-1893
Fax 777-9195

- Close to the Queen Street West Village
- 87 suites $60–$65, children under 12 free
- Parking $1.50 per day
- Suites include kitchenettes and cable TV
- Cribs available
- No babysitting
- No non-smoking floors
- No pets
- Coin-op laundry
- Disabled access
- No restaurant or recreational facilities

Ashton Manor Group

88 Isabella Street
Toronto ON M4Y 1N5
Tel 925-5529 Fax 925-1780

- Two downtown locations on Isabella Street and on Huntley Street, one midtown location on Davisville Avenue
- Rates from $60–$85, depending on location; 3-night minimum stay, children under 12 free
- CAA discounts sometimes available
- Apartments have cable TV, kitchens, fridges, stoves; some have dishwashers, some have microwaves
- Cribs available
- Some babysitting (depends on location)
- No non-smoking floors
- Disabled access
- No pets
- Coin-op laundry
- No restaurants
- Indoor pools at Davisville and Huntley locations

Bed and breakfast homes

These private houses offer a homey atmosphere and usually their hosts are a fount of

37

information on the city; however, only some B & Bs are suitable for children, especially younger ones. Individual home owners choose whether or not to accept children, based on the kids' ages, numbers, and what rooms they have available at the time you are booking.

Amenities and regulations vary at B & Bs and depend very much on how a host operates his or her home. Some allow pets but not smokers. Some are

Babysitting

For many parents, one of the highlights of a trip away from home is the chance to spend a little time together, *sans* children. Something as simple as a quiet meal and a stroll, and the opportunity to have an uninterrupted conversation, is the stuff that dreams are made of if you're raising young children.

Most hotels and other accommodations will arrange babysitting for guests through licensed city agencies, at the same rates these agencies normally charge for home babysitting. For your own peace of mind, you may prefer to call the agencies yourself, so that you can talk to the operators and request the sort of sitter who will best suit your family. The following three agencies are all licensed and regulated by the Ontario government.

Active Home Services
785-4818

On 24 hours' notice, Active Home Services can provide experienced sitters throughout Metro. Rates are $7.50 per hour for one child, an additional 50¢ per hour per additional child (for children in the same family), with a four-hour minimum. Families are also charged a $10 transportation charge before 1 am, rising to $20 after 1 am. All of the sitters are non-smokers, and many have first-aid training. You can arrange to have the sitter take your kids on daytime outings to parks or attractions (by public transit only); the only activities they won't supervise are swimming and baths. If your child requires any medication, you must leave written directions for its administration.

happy to let guests use their laundry facilities or their kitchens to heat snacks and bottles; for others these areas are strictly off limits to visitors. At some B & Bs you may find yourself sharing a bathroom with other guests; if you want a private bath, make this clear when you book.

While the city has scores of bed and breakfast homes, many hosts prefer not to take reservations directly, but rather to use the services of an

Christopher Robin Service
289-4430

This agency has been in business for 40 years, and can usually provide sitters on two hours' notice. Rates are $30 for the minimum first three hours and $7 per hour thereafter. If you are out till after 1 am, you will be charged $6 for the sitter's transportation. Daytime outings can also be arranged (with the customary restriction on swimming). All sitters have first-aid training. Written directions for any medication must be left with the sitter.

Kids Are Us
1107 Queen Street East
406-6759

This storefront childcare business operated by a mother-and-daughter team welcomes kids from infants up to age eight. Children must come to the store, so it's likely that they will be sharing the toys and play equipment (sand table, climber, slide) with playmates. The Kids Are Us operators abide by the government's rules about adult-child ratios, so it's best to phone and book a time to be sure of a spot, although spur-of-the-moment arrangements can often be made.

The storefront drop-in service is open weekdays between 8:30 am and 4:30 pm. Saturday care is available, but three days' notice is usually required. The storefront provides snacks, but youngsters must bring their own lunches. The operators, who both have early childhood education and first-aid training, will bottle-feed babies on demand. Rates are $5 per hour for one child and an additional $3 per hour per additional child (for children in the same family).

association. The following B & B associations represent a variety of homes that will welcome your whole family.

- **Bed and Breakfast Homes of Toronto**
  P.O. Box 46093
  College Park Post Office
  Toronto ON M5B 2L8
  Tel 363-6362

This organization is a co-op of independent B & B owners. They are happy to mail out their brochure of homes, which guests can contact individually. Their homes are located mainly in central Toronto and a few offer self-contained "unhosted" suites that are suitable for families. Rates range from $55 to $95 a night. Sometimes discounts are offered for longer stays.

- **Toronto Bed & Breakfast Association**
  P.O. Box 269
  253 College Street
  Toronto ON M5T 1R5
  Tel 588-8800 or 596-1118
  Fax 977-2601

This organization represents 20 homes (all located close to subway stations) which accept bookings only through the association. Rates run between $70 and $85 a night, and some homes have cribs on hand. The association can also make weekly and monthly reservations for furnished bachelor and one-bedroom apartments, with a daily double occupancy rate of $50 to $95.

- **Downtown Toronto Association of Bed and Breakfast Guest Houses**
  P.O. Box 190 Station "B"
  Toronto ON M5T 2W1
  Tel 368-1420 Fax 368-1653

This organization represents 25 homes in the area bounded by St. Clair Avenue, the Beaches, and the Canadian National Exhibition grounds. Rates run between $55 and $80 a night, and a few homes have self-contained apartments. Most offer laundry facilities, for which there may be a charge; none accept pets. Cribs and playpens are available at some homes. Reservations are accepted only through the association, which makes every effort to match families with homes that serve their needs.

One independent home that gladly welcomes families with children is:

At Balmy Beach in the Beaches

274 Waverley Road
Toronto ON M4L 3T6
Tel and Fax 690-8254

Host Ruth Hennigan offers a one-bedroom, air-conditioned, self-contained apartment unit with complete kitchen facilities for the bargain rate of $75 per night. Her own four teenaged and preteen children are delighted to have visiting kids, and the Beaches location is close to the lake, the boardwalk, Queen Street East shops and restaurants, and parks with lots of recreational facilities. Public transit along Queen Street takes about 30 minutes to reach downtown. Guests with babies are welcome but must provide their own portacrib.

Campgrounds

Camping within Metro is limited, but if you're willing to make a longer drive, there are campgrounds in conservation areas and provincial parks on the city's periphery. Call the Ontario Ministry of Culture and Recreation (314-0944) for more information.

Glen Rouge Campgrounds

**7540 Kingston Road
(Highway 2 and Port Union Road)
Tel 392-2541 or 392-2554
Fax 392-3350**

- Operated by Metropolitan Toronto Parks and Property.
- Located close to the Metro Toronto Zoo and the Glen Rouge Park, a 40-minute car ride to downtown
- Open Victoria Day weekend through Thanksgiving, but regarded as a "tourist stop-over," i.e., not many amenities
- 126 sites: 89 serviced sites $22; unserviced sites $16
- Hot water, toilets, and showers available
- No laundry facilities, no snack bar or groceries
- Pets on leashes are permitted
- Maximum stay is 9 days

Indian Line Tourist Campground

**7625 Finch Avenue
West off Highway 427
905-678-1233**

- Operated by Metropolitan Toronto & Region Conservation Authority
- Located close to the Wild Water Kingdom and 20 minutes by car from Paramount Canada's Wonderland, 40-minute car ride to downtown
- Open May 1 through October 15
- 220 sites: unserviced sites $15, serviced sites $19

41

- Hot water, toilets, and showers available
- Coin-op laundry, grocery store near campground, children's playground
- Outdoor pool, on-site fishing
- Pets on leashes are permitted

College residences

Renting accommodations in university and college residences during the summer when most students are away can be a relatively inexpensive alternative for families. At both Glendon and Scarborough Colleges, visitors have the added pleasure of staying in beautiful natural settings with expansive walking and playing areas, while the downtown residences are located close to attractions and public transit.

Downtown residences

Neill-Wycik College Hotel

Ryerson Polytechnic University
96 Gerrard Street East
Toronto ON M5B 1G7
Tel 977-2320 1-800-268-4358
Fax 977-2809

- 10-minute walk to Dundas Station and Eaton Centre
- Tourist rooms available May through August
- 300 rooms, family rooms (2 single beds plus 3 cots) $47; up to 2 children under 17 free, additional children $10
- Shared washroom and kitchen facilities
- Cribs available
- No babysitting
- Disabled access
- No non-smoking floors
- No pets
- Coin-op laundry
- TV lounge on top floor
- No phone or air-conditioning
- Cafeteria
- Sauna and roof deck

Victoria University

University of Toronto
140 Charles Street West
Toronto ON M5S 1K8
Tel 585-4524 Fax 585-4530

- Excellent location close to the Royal Ontario Museum and Bloor-Yorkville
- Tourist rooms available May 7 to August 27
- 600 rooms (twin beds only), $60; $12 per child (maximum 2 children); rate includes full breakfast
- Shared kitchen and washroom facilities

- No parking facilities though public lot nearby
- No TV, phone, or air-conditioning in rooms
- No cribs
- Cots available
- No babysitting
- Limited disabled access
- No non-smoking floors
- No pets
- Coin-op laundry
- Cafeteria
- Tennis courts

Suburban campuses

Glendon College
York University
2275 Bayview Avenue
Toronto ON M4N 3M6
Tel 487-6798
Fax 487-6793

- North Toronto location, 30 minutes to downtown by car; public transit at university entrance
- Tourist rooms available from beginning of May to August 26
- 222 rooms $62, cots available for $7
- Two parking lots; rates $4.50 and $8 per day, free on weekends
- No radios or TVs in rooms
- No air-conditioning
- Shared washroom facilities
- Kitchen access for long stays only
- Some babysitting
- First-floor disabled access
- Non-smoking building except for designated areas
- No pets
- Coin-op laundry
- Cafeteria open 8 am–3 pm weekdays
- Limited recreational facilities available for a charge

43

Hospitality York

York University
4700 Keele Street
North York ON M3J 1P3
Tel 736-5020 Fax 736-5648

- Near Black Creek Pioneer Village and Paramount Canada's Wonderland, 50 minutes to downtown by car; over 60 minutes to downtown by bus and subway
- Tourist accommodation available May through August
- 66 residence suites (5 bedrooms, 2 baths, kitchen) $160, maximum occupancy of 6 people
- Apartments range from bachelors to 2 bedrooms for $700 to $1100 per month; short-term rental is limited
- Parking $4.50 per day
- Some air-conditioning
- Cots available, no cribs
- Babysitting available at campus daycare (24 hours' notice required); $8.50 for 2 hours, $40.25 per day
- Disabled access
- No non-smoking units
- Pets permitted in some accommodation areas
- Coin-op laundry
- On-site shops, banking, fast-food outlets, pool, and cafeteria

Scarborough College

University of Toronto
1265 Military Trail
Scarborough ON M1C 1A4
Tel 287-7369 Fax 287-7667

- Close to the Metro Zoo, on an extensive ravine park system, 50 minutes to downtown by car, over 60 minutes to downtown by bus and subway
- Tourist accommodation available mid-May through August
- 81 units (374 beds) divided between 4- and 6-person townhouses with fully equipped kitchens, $140 for minimum 2-night stay; $65 for each additional night, $400 per week, children under 18 free
- Parking included
- No cribs or cots
- No babysitting
- No disabled access
- No non-smoking units
- No pets
- Coin-op laundry
- Cafeteria open 8 am–4 pm weekdays
- Recreation centre (no pool) for adults only

Hotels

Most kids love staying in hotels, which the younger ones happily treat like high-rise playgrounds: elevators to ride, halls to race down, beds to jump on. Many hotels have gotten wise to the needs of their younger guests and provide special facilities or programs for kids, which may include on-site childcare or even children's entertainment and excursions during prime periods like March Break. As always, ask what's available before you book. Those little extras can add considerably to your family's enjoyment.

Hotel rates may vary throughout the year, depending on availability and competition. When you call to reserve, *never* accept the first rate (sometimes called the "rack" rate) you are offered; ask if there are any special family discounts, weekend or corporate rates, special promotions, or affiliation discounts (such as automobile associations), and be persistent. There are almost always savings available.

The listings below focus on downtown and midtown hotels. A few suburban hotels that offer suites or have an attractive location are also included. If you want information on other suburban hotels or airport hotels, consult the accommodation services mentioned on page 35.

Toronto's best hotels for families

Delta Chelsea Inn ✱

33 Gerrard Street West
Toronto ON M5G 1Z4
Tel 595-1975
Can: 1-800-268-1133
US: 1-800-877-1133
Fax 585-4302

Close to the Eaton Centre and City Hall, the mid-priced Delta Chelsea Inn is one of a handful of hotels offering extensive services and discounts specifically for families. Ask for their family rate, a reduction in the regular room rate of nearly 50 percent. Their Children's Creative Centre is open seven days a week year-round, offering supervised activities for children aged 3 1/2 to 12 ($5 for two half-hour visits per day). There is also a video games room, which is appealing to older kids.

- 1600 rooms and suites, deluxe rooms from $102 for families, kitchenette rooms $107 for families; 1-bedroom or 2-bedroom suite with kitchen $240–$300 (no discounts available); children under 18 free
- CAA discount
- Parking $15 per night
- Rooms include cable TV, VCR, and movies for rent
- Cribs available
- Babysitting available
- Disabled access
- Non-smoking floors
- Pets permitted, deposit required
- Coin-op laundry
- 2 restaurants, 1 cafeteria-style, children's menu, children under 6 years eat free, kids aged 6–12 eat for half-price
- 2 pools (1 family pool)
- Adults-only health club

Four Seasons Hotel ✱

21 Avenue Road
Toronto ON M5R 2G1
Tel 964-0411
Can: 1-800-268-6282
US: 1-800-332-3442
Fax 964-2301

In the heart of Yorkville, near the Royal Ontario Museum, the Four Seasons is a luxury-class hotel that offers a "Toronto Kids" program for its younger guests. Accommodations include many special touches like childproof rooms with stepstools and miniature furniture, kids' bathrobes, and a cookies-and-milk turn-down service. Parents with babies will appreciate the availability of high chairs, bottle warmers, diapers, and baby-care supplies. Families can borrow video game units, and for no extra charge bicycles are available for cruising the nearby Yorkville neighbourhood and points beyond.

- 210 rooms, 170 suites; rates start at $260, children under 18 free

- No CAA discount
- Parking $18 per day, in and out privileges
- Rooms include minifridges, pay TV, VCRs for rent
- Babysitting available
- Disabled access
- Non-smoking floors
- Pets permitted
- Hotel valet laundry service
- 4 restaurants, children's menu
- Heated year-round indoor/outdoor pool
- Supervised children permitted in sauna and whirlpool

Four Seasons Inn on the Park ✱

1100 Eglinton Avenue East
North York ON M3C 1H8
Tel 444-2561
Can: 1-800-268-6282
US: 1-800-332-3442
Fax 446-3308

Located on 243 hectares (600 acres) of parkland with jogging, nature, and bike trails, 20 minutes to downtown by car, 40 minutes by TTC. This suburban hotel caters to families with a supervised "Innkidz" program for children five to twelve years old, seven days a week in summer and on weekends during the rest of the year. Games, arts and crafts, and movies entertain the kids, along with an outdoor playground and two pools.

- 541 rooms $100–$199, ask for weekend specials; 27 one-bedroom suites $230–$260 (no kitchenettes); children under 18 free
- Free parking
- Rooms include minifridges and cable TV with pay-per-view movies; VCRs for rent
- Cribs available

- Babysitting available
- Disabled access
- Non-smoking floors
- Some pet restrictions
- Hotel laundry service
- Several restaurants, children's menus
- Video games room
- Indoor and outdoor pools, sauna, whirlpool, tennis courts

Howard Johnson Plaza-Hotel – Downtown ✱

475 Yonge Street
Toronto ON M4Y 1X7
Tel 924-0611 1-800-446-4656
Fax 924-5061

Although this centrally located hotel doesn't have extensive facilities for kids, it does offer one big plus: complimentary passes to the downtown YMCA, which is right around the corner and has every activity going for families (see page 148), including inexpensive babysitting and a health-conscious cafeteria.

- 328 rooms from $99, children under 18 free
- CAA discount
- Parking $12 per day, in and out privileges
- Rooms include cable TV with pay-per-view movies

- Children can sign out video games at front desk
- Cribs and cots available
- Babysitting available
- Non-smoking floors
- No pets
- Hotel laundry service
- Howard Johnson restaurant in hotel, children's menu
- Adult-only exercise room
- Children receive complimentary gift package at check-in
- 10-minute walk to Bloor-Yorkville

Park Plaza Hotel ✱

4 Avenue Road
Toronto ON M5R 2E8
Tel 924-5471 1-800-268-4927
Fax 924-4933

This well-established hotel offers a great location, close to the city's best shopping. Family Bed and Breakfast Specials (depending on availability) reduce the regular room rate to $115 on weekdays and $99 on weekends. During the tourist season from Victoria Day to Labour Day, the hotel offers a Children's Activity Centre, open every day, with supervised crafts and other activities, all free. During the rest of the year, half-day babysitting is offered on Sundays, so that parents can enjoy brunch at the hotel restaurant. Books and games are available from the concierge, and gift packs are given to children on arrival.

- 264 rooms $180–$260, 40 suites $240, children under 18 free
- CAA discount
- Parking $17 per day, in and out privileges
- Rooms include minibars, cable TV with pay-per-view movies and complimentary Disney Channel; movie rentals can be arranged
- Cribs available
- Babysitting available
- Disabled access
- Non-smoking floors
- Small pets allowed
- Hotel laundry service
- Coin-op laundry 5 minutes away
- 2 restaurants, children under 12 eat for half-price
- Supervised children allowed in exercise room

Toronto Prince Hotel ✱

900 York Mills Road
North York ON M3B 3H2
Tel 444-2511
Can: 1-800-268-7677
US: 1-800-323-7500
Fax 444-9597

This suburban hotel, surround-ed by green space and near walking and hiking trails, offers lots for kids and active families: three tennis courts, an outdoor pool, a nine-hole putting green, a shuffleboard court, and a children's outdoor play area. Indoors there is a climbing gym with slide, billiards table, and separate children's room with art supplies and games. Children are allowed in the sauna, whirlpool, and exercise room. During peak family travel times like March Break, special children's programs are usually scheduled. A large shopping mall, Fairview, is a five-minute drive away.

- 176 rooms $110–$210 regular rates, $99–$130 weekend rates (must be negotiated); 10 suites $200–$700, children under 18 free
- CAA discount
- Parking free
- Rooms include minifridges and cable TV with pay-per-view movies
- Cribs available
- Babysitting available
- Disabled access
- Non-smoking floors
- No pets
- Hotel laundry service
- 3 restaurants, children's menus

Westin Harbour Castle ✱

1 Harbour Square
Toronto ON M5J 1A6
Tel 869-1600 1-800-228-3000
Fax 361-7448

This waterfront hotel boasts spectacular views and a great location right beside the ferry docks for Toronto Islands, and a five-minute walk from Harbourfront and Metro's downtown core. The Harbour Castle sponsors a "Westin Kids' Club," which includes a separate check-in for children, who receive a club kit with products and activities geared to their age level. During their stay, kids can participate in arts and crafts or watch movies in a supervised children's activity room. Parents will be grateful for the free room-safety kit, available on check-in, and for the other items — bed rails, potty seats, strollers, high chairs, night lights — that can be borrowed. The hotel laundry service even offers a special kids' rate.

- 980 rooms $109–$195, children under 18 free
- CAA discount
- Valet parking $17.75 per day, also nearby public parking
- Rooms include cable TV with

pay-per-view movies and minibars
- Cribs available
- Babysitting available
- Disabled access
- Non-smoking floors
- Pets allowed
- 3 restaurants, children's menus (meals can be ordered in advance to reduce waiting); children under 12 eat free (2 children per adult)
- Indoor pool, sauna, whirlpool open to supervised children

Downtown hotels

Best Western Chestnut Park Hotel

108 Chestnut Street
Toronto ON M5G 1R3
Tel 977-5000
Can: 1-800-668-6600
US: 1-800-528-1234
Fax 977-9513

- Close to the Art Gallery of Ontario, City Hall, the Eaton Centre, and the Queen Street West Village
- 491 rooms from $99, children under 18 free
- CAA discount
- Parking $16 per day, in and out privileges
- Rooms include colour TV with movie channel and minibars
- Cribs available
- Babysitting available
- Disabled access
- Non-smoking floors
- Pets allowed
- Hotel laundry service
- 2 restaurants, no children's menu
- Indoor pool, whirlpool, sauna, and exercise room

Best Western Primrose Hotel

111 Carlton Street
Toronto ON M5B 2G3
Tel 977-8000 1-800-268-8082
Fax 977-6323

- Close to Maple Leaf Gardens
- 350 rooms from $75, breakfast included; 4 suites $150 (no kitchen facilities); children under 18 free
- CAA discount
- Parking $10 per day
- Rooms include cable TV with

pay-per-view movies
- Limited number of minifridges may be booked in advance
- Cribs available
- Babysitting available
- Disabled access
- Non-smoking floors
- No pets
- Hotel laundry service
- 2 restaurants
- Outdoor pool (seasonal), 2 saunas

Bond Place Hotel

65 Dundas Street East
Toronto ON M5B 2G8
Tel 362-6061
1-800-268-9390
Fax 360-6406

- Close to the Eaton Centre
- 286 rooms $69–$119, children under 14 free
- Occasional package rates offered
- CAA discount
- Parking $11 per day, in and out privileges
- Rooms include cable TV with pay-per-view movies
- Cribs available
- Babysitting available
- Disabled access
- No pets
- Hotel laundry service
- Restaurant, no children's menu

Camberley Club Hotel

40 King Street West
Toronto ON M5H 3Y2
Tel 947-9025
1-800-866-ROOM
Fax 947-0622

- Close to SkyDome, CN Tower, and the theatre district
- 54 suites without kitchen facilities $135–$160 weekends, $210–$270 weekdays; rates include continental breakfast, afternoon tea, and hors d'oeuvres; children under 12 free, additional charge of $10 for children aged 12–18
- CAA discount
- Parking $20 per day weekdays, in and out privileges; $4.50 per half-hour on weekends
- All suites include Jacuzzis and 2 TVs with remotes and VCRs; free videos from hotel library
- Cribs available
- Babysitting available
- Disabled access
- Non-smoking rooms only
- No pets
- Hotel laundry service
- Restaurant, no children's menu
- Adult guests may use the athletic facilities of the (offsite) Adelaide Club

Cambridge Suites Hotel

15 Richmond Street East
Toronto ON M5C 1N2
Tel 368-1990
Can & US: 1-800-463-1990
Fax 601-3753

- Close to the Eaton Centre and City Hall
- 228 suites $125–$250, $80 per night for stays over 30 days, continental breakfast included, children under 18 free
- CAA discount
- Parking $14 per weekday, free on weekends
- Suites include minifridge, microwave, dishes, sink, and coffee machine, cable TV with pay-per-view movies
- Cribs available
- Babysitting available
- Disabled access
- Non-smoking floors
- Pets allowed, deposit required
- Coin-op laundry
- Restaurant
- Supervised children allowed in exercise room

Comfort Hotel

15 Charles Street East
Toronto ON M4Y 1S1

Tel 924-1222 Fax 927-1369
1-800-228-5050 (This toll-free
number will connect you to a
USA-based reservation service
which can get you a discounted
rate at the Comfort Hotel — one
that you might not receive if
you call the hotel directly.)

- Close to Bloor-Yorkville
- 108 rooms $90, 7 suites
  $89– $99, children under
  18 free
- Suites include sitting room
  but no extra sleeping
  accommodation
- CAA discount
- Limited parking $8 per day
- Rooms include cable TV
- Cribs available
- No babysitting
- No disabled access
- Non-smoking floors
- No pets
- Hotel laundry service
- Restaurant, no children's
  menu
- Adults-only recreation
  facilities

Crowne Plaza Toronto Centre

225 Front Street West
Toronto ON M5V 2X3
Tel 597-1400 1-800-465-4329
Fax 597-8128

- Close to SkyDome, the CN
  Tower, and the theatre district

- 587 rooms and suites; rooms
  $89–$169; junior, 1-bedroom,
  and 2-bedroom suites
  $165–$375; children under
  18 free
- CAA discount
- Parking $21 per day
- Rooms include cable TV with
  pay-per-view movies and
  coffeemakers
- Cribs available, cots
  $15 extra
- Babysitting available
- Disabled access
- Non-smoking floors
- No pets
- Hotel laundry service
- 2 restaurants, children's
  menu, children under 12
  eat free
- Indoor swimming pool,
  sauna, whirlpool,
  sundeck

Days Inn Toronto Downtown

30 Carlton Street
Toronto ON M5B 2E9
Tel 977-6655 1-800-325-2525
Fax 977-0502

- Close to Maple Leaf
  Gardens
- 536 rooms $69–$89, children
  under 18 free
- CAA discount
- Underground parking
  $10 per day

- Rooms include cable TV and pay-per-view movies; many rooms include minifridges
- Cribs available
- No babysitting
- No disabled access
- Non-smoking floors
- Some restrictions on pets
- Coin-op laundry
- 2 restaurants, no children's menu
- Indoor pool and sauna

- Babysitting available
- Disabled access
- Non-smoking floors
- No pets
- Hotel laundry service
- 3 restaurants, children under 18 eat free (with parents)
- Supervised, heated outdoor rooftop pool with pool toys; sauna
- Supervised children's activities on weekends during summer

Holiday Inn on King

370 King Street West
Toronto ON M5V 1J9
Tel 599-4000 1-800-HOLIDAY
Fax 599-7394

- Close to SkyDome, the CN Tower, and the theatre district
- 426 rooms $115–$190, children under 18 free
- CAA discount
- Underground parking $11 per day, in and out privileges
- Rooms include cable TV with pay-per-view movies; some rooms equipped with wet bars
- Some suites include fridges and sitting rooms with a pull-out couch
- Cribs available

Hotel Inter-Continental Toronto

220 Bloor Street West
Toronto ON M5S 1T8
Tel 960-5200 1-800-327-0200
Fax 960-8269

- Close to Bloor-Yorkville and the Royal Ontario Museum
- 209 rooms $165–$205, 9 suites (no kitchenettes) $320; children under 12 free
- CAA discount
- Parking $13 per day, no in and out privileges
- Rooms include cable TV and minibars; movie rentals available
- Cribs available, cots $20 per day
- Babysitting available
- Disabled access
- Non-smoking floors

- Pets allowed
- Hotel laundry service
- Restaurant, children's menu
- Supervised children allowed in indoor pool and fitness room

Hotel Plaza II

90 Bloor Street East
Toronto ON M4W 1A7
Tel 961-8000 1-800-267-6116
Fax 961-4635

- Close to Bloor-Yorkville
- 255 rooms $105–$200; weekend reductions, depending on room availability; 17 suites $250 (no kitchen facilities, minibars only); children under 18 free; inquire about special weekend packages
- CAA discount
- Valet parking $17 per day, in and out privileges
- Rooms include cable TV with pay-per-view movies
- Minibars on request
- Cribs available
- Babysitting available
- Disabled access
- Non-smoking floors
- Some restrictions on pets
- Hotel laundry service
- Restaurant, half-portions for children are served
- Complimentary passes to Bloor Park Health Club

The King Edward Hotel

37 King Street East
Toronto ON M5C 1E9
Tel 863-9700 1-800-225-5843
Fax 367-5515

- Close to the Hockey Hall of Fame, St. Lawrence Market, and theatre district
- 312 rooms from $224, suites from $300 (no kitchen facilities), children under 18 free
- Suites and rooms include minibars and cable TVs with pay-per-view movies
- Cribs available
- Babysitting available
- Disabled access
- Non-smoking floors
- No pets
- Hotel laundry service
- 3 restaurants, children's

menu; special kids' price for Sunday brunch

- Small exercise room, Jacuzzi

Novotel Toronto Centre

45 The Esplanade
Toronto ON M5E 1W2
Tel 367-8900 1-800-668-6835
Fax 360-8285

- Close to the CN Tower, SkyDome, and theatre district
- 266 rooms $99–$159, children under 18 free
- CAA discount
- Rooms include cable TV with pay-per-view movies
- Cribs available
- No babysitting
- Disabled access
- Non-smoking floors
- No pets
- Hotel laundry service
- Restaurant, no children's menu
- Indoor pool and health club (sauna, whirlpool), super-vised children may visit

Quality Hotel by Journey's End

111 Lombard Street
Toronto ON M5C 2T9
Tel 367-5555 1-800-221-2222
Fax 367-3470

- Close to the St. Lawrence Market, Hockey Hall of

Fame, and theatre district

- 194 rooms $85 weekdays, $59 weekends; children under 19 free
- CAA discount
- Parking $9.75 per day, in and out privileges
- Rooms include cable TV with pay-per-view movies
- Cribs available
- No babysitting available
- Disabled access
- Non-smoking floors
- Pets permitted on request
- Hotel laundry service
- No restaurant

Radisson Plaza Hotel Admiral Toronto–Harbourfront

249 Queen's Quay West
Toronto ON M5J 2N5
Tel 203-3333 1-800-333-3333
Fax 203-3100

- Close to Harbourfront, the theatre district, and the Hockey Hall of Fame
- 157 rooms $140 for standard room, $79–$99 promotional rate sometimes available; 17 suites $270 (without kitchen facilities); children under 18 free
- CAA discount
- Parking $12.50 per day, in and out privileges

- Rooms include cable TV with pay-per-view movies and minibars
- Cribs available
- Babysitting available
- Disabled access
- Non-smoking floors
- No pets
- Hotel laundry service
- 2 restaurants, children's menu
- Outdoor pool and whirlpool
- Guests may use the nearby SkyDome Health Club ($10 fee per visit)

Royal York Hotel

100 Front Street West
Toronto ON M5J 1E3
Tel 368-2511
Can & US: 1-800-441-1414
Fax 368-2884

- Close to the CN Tower, SkyDome, the theatre district, and the Hockey Hall of Fame
- 1375 rooms $155–$219, weekend rates from $109 if available; children under 17 free
- CAA discount
- Parking $17 per weekday, $10 maximum per weekend
- Rooms include cable TV with pay-per-view movies, movie and VCR rental
- Minifridges available on request

- Cribs available
- Babysitting available
- Disabled access
- Non-smoking floors
- No pets
- Hotel laundry service
- 9 restaurants, children's menu
- Indoor pool, separate children's wading pool, Jacuzzi, sauna, and exercise room

Sheraton Centre Toronto Hotel and Towers

123 Queen Street West
Toronto ON M5H 2M9
Tel 361-1000 1-800-325-3535
Fax 947-4801

- Close to City Hall, Queen Street West Village, and the Eaton Centre
- 1382 rooms from $115,

weekend rates available;
over 100 suites (no kitchen
facilities) $350–$700; children
under 18 free
- CAA discount
- Parking $20 per day
- Rooms equipped with TVs,
  movie channel, minibars
- Cribs available
- Babysitting available
- Disabled access
- Non-smoking floors
- No pets
- Hotel laundry service
- 4 restaurants, children's
  menu
- Outdoor/indoor pool, supervised children permitted
  in exercise room, games
  room with Ping Pong table
  by pool

SkyDome Hotel

1 Blue Jays Way
Toronto ON M5V 1J4
Tel 360-7100
1-800-441-1414
Fax 341-5090
- Close to the CN Tower and
  the theatre district
- 346 rooms from $109;
  68 suites; some rooms and
  suites overlook the SkyDome
  playing field
- CAA discount
- Parking $16 per day, no in
  and out privileges

- Suites and rooms include
  cable TV with pay-per-view
  movies, minibars, coffee-
  makers, and hairdryers;
  some suites include Jacuzzis,
  microwaves, and full-sized
  fridges
- Cribs available
- Babysitting available
- Disabled access
- Non-smoking floors
- Pets allowed
- Hotel laundry service
- Several restaurants,
  including McDonald's
- Indoor pool

Sutton Place Grande Hotel

955 Bay Street
Toronto ON M5S 2A2
Tel 924-9221 1-800-268-3790
Fax 924-1778
- 10-minute walk to Bloor-
  Yorkville, close to Queen's
  Park and the University of
  Toronto
- 208 rooms $155–$285
  weekdays, $160 weekends;
  weekend rates include
  breakfast and parking;
  72 1-, 2-, 3-bedroom suites
  (some with full kitchens) up
  to $700, with discount rates
  sometimes available;
  children under 18 free
- CAA discount

- Parking $16 per day
- Rooms include cable TV with pay-per-view movies
- Cribs available
- Babysitting available
- Disabled access
- Non-smoking floors
- Pets allowed
- Hotel laundry service
- 2 restaurants, no children's menu
- Indoor pool with large sundeck, sauna; supervised children permitted in exercise room

Toronto Colony Hotel

89 Chestnut Street
Toronto ON M5G 1R1
Tel 977-0707 1-800-854-7854
Fax 585-3157

- Close to the Art Gallery of Ontario, City Hall, the Eaton Centre, and the Queen Street West Village
- 715 rooms from $114 (regular rate), $89–$124 (promotional rate), suites (no kitchen facilities) $125, a 10 percent discount for stays over one week, children under 18 free
- CAA discount
- Parking $12 per day
- Suites and rooms include minifridges, and cable TV with pay-per-view movies,

microwaves available on request
- Cribs available
- Babysitting available
- Disabled access
- Non-smoking floors
- Pets allowed
- Hotel laundry service
- Restaurant, children under 12 eat free
- Indoor and outdoor pools
- Supervised children allowed in fitness centre, Jacuzzi

Toronto Hilton Hotel

145 Richmond Street West
Toronto ON M5H 2L2
Tel 869-3456 1-800-445-8667
Fax 869-3187

- Close to City Hall, the Eaton Centre, and the Queen Street West Village
- 601 rooms $145–$215, children under 18 free
- CAA discount
- Parking $17 per weekday, $12 weekends; in and out privileges
- Rooms include cable TV with pay-per-view movies, and minibars
- Cribs available
- Babysitting available
- Disabled access
- Non-smoking floors
- Pets under 9 kilograms

(20 lbs) allowed but must be with owner at all times

- Hotel laundry service
- Restaurant, children under 12 eat free
- Heated indoor/outdoor pool
- Accompanied children permitted in fitness room, Jacuzzi, whirlpool and sauna

Midtown hotels

Bradgate Arms

54 Foxbar Road
Toronto ON M4V 2G6
Tel 968-1331   1-800-268-7171
Fax 968-3743

- Midtown location, quiet residential area; 5 minutes by streetcar to St. Clair Station
- 110 rooms $112 weekdays, $102 weekends; 5 suites with wet bar $125 weekdays, $110 weekends; discounts for stays over 8 days; children under 18 free
- No CAA discounts
- Free parking (subject to availability)
- Rooms include TVs with movie channel
- Minifridges available on request
- Cribs available
- Babysitting available
- Disabled access

- Non-smoking floors
- No pets
- Hotel laundry service
- Restaurant, no children's menu
- Supervised children allowed in exercise room and whirlpool
- Offsite privileges at Lakeshore Mayfair racquet club (guests must pay court fees and equipment rentals)

Best Western Roehampton Hotel

808 Mount Pleasant Road
Toronto ON M4P 2L2
Tel 487-5101   1-800-387-8899
Fax 487-5390

- Midtown residential area, 10-minute walk to Eglinton Station
- 101 rooms $79–$99, children under 18 free
- CAA discount
- Parking $6.45 per day, in and out privileges
- Rooms include cable TV with pay-per-view movies, most have minifridges
- Cribs available
- Babysitting available (24 hours' notice)
- Disabled access
- Non-smoking floors

- Pets allowed
- Hotel laundry service
- No restaurant, bar only
- Heated outdoor pool

Suburban hotels

Embassy Suites Hotel – Toronto/ Markham

8500 Warden Avenue
Markham ON L6G 1A5
Tel 905-470-8500
1-800-668-8800
Fax 905-477-8611

- Northerly suburban location; 45 minutes by car to downtown
- 332 suites from $165 weekdays, $109 weekends; complimentary buffet breakfast; children under 12 free; additional charge of $20 per child over 12
- CAA discounts
- Free parking
- All suites have 2 TVs with pay-per-view movies, pull-out couches in second room, coffeemakers and microwaves on request, and most have minifridges
- Cribs available
- Babysitting available
- Non-smoking floors

- No pets
- Coin-op laundry
- Restaurant, no children's menu
- Indoor pool
- Health club, with some restrictions on children
- Games room (shuffleboard, billiard table, pinball)

The Guild Inn

201 Guildwood Parkway
Scarborough ON M1E 1P6
Tel 261-3331
Can: 1-800-268-1133
US: 1-800-877-1133
Fax 261-5675

- Historic building, close to Scarborough Bluffs; 45-minute drive to downtown
- 90 rooms $75, 6 suites $115, children under 18 free
- CAA discount
- Free parking
- Rooms include colour TV
- Some suites with pull-out couches in living room
- Cribs available
- No babysitting
- Disabled access
- Non-smoking rooms
- Pets allowed
- Hotel laundry service
- Heated outdoor pool and tennis court, exercise room, Ping Pong table

61

4: Kids just wanna have fun: Toronto's Top 10 family attractions

In a city as rich in diversions as Toronto, it's a challenge to pick the Top 10. Popularity is one measure, and all of the sites described here have wowed millions of visitors over the years. These are the best known of the city's attractions, some world famous and rightly so. They are listed in alphabetical order, and those that are especially worthy of a visit win the teddy bear stamp of approval.

1. Casa Loma ✱

Where? 1 Austin Terrace
923-1171
TTC: Take the St. Clair streetcar to Spadina Road and walk south
When? 10 am–4 pm daily
How much? $8 for adults, $4.50 for children 6-16, children under 6 free
How long? 2 hours

Extras: Snackbar, gift shop; admission price includes access to outstanding gardens

While Toronto may have no Walt Disney World, it does have an "authentic" castle where kids can act out their fantasies of knights and ladies from a time long ago.

"The Castle on the Hill" has

been a Toronto landmark since 1914, when it was constructed by Sir Henry Pellatt, a local financier who earned a vast fortune in railways and electricity. More lavish than any home built in the city before or since, Casa Loma cost $3.5 million and contained furnishings worth another $1.5 million — in 1914 dollars! Sir Henry lived in the castle for a mere nine years; he was forced to leave and to see his belongings auctioned off at fire-sale prices after a dramatic reversal wiped out his fortune. It's estimated that he amassed over $17 million during his lifetime; when he died in 1939, he was worth a paltry $35,000.

In his heyday, Sir Henry visited Europe and returned from his travels with a head full of grandiose plans to copy the great castles he had seen. He commissioned a 98-room hodgepodge of architectural styles that impressed the locals and surpassed the efforts of just about every other millionaire in North America at that time. Crenellated towers, soaring battlements, sweeping terraces, underground tunnels, and secret passageways —

Casa Loma has them all.

Now operated by the Kiwanis Club of Casa Loma as a tourist attraction and events facility, most of the castle's major rooms are open to the public. For kids, the must-sees are Sir Henry's study on the main floor, which has a hidden door on either side of the fireplace; Sir Henry's marble bathroom on the second floor with its body-surrounding multi-nozzled shower; the third-floor towers, which are fun to climb and offer spectacular views; and the unfinished swimming pool in the basement, which has a deliciously spooky atmosphere.

No youngster will want to pass up the 300-metre (800-foot) "secret" tunnel to the stables north of the castle, where even Sir Henry's horses lived luxuriously. Each one had a mahogany stall, monogrammed in 18-karat gold with its occupant's name.

Every year from December through New Year's Day, Casa Loma is extravagantly decorated according to a theme, such as Alice in Wonderland or Scrooge's Christmas, with lots of special activities for kids and the city's biggest indoor Christmas tree. This is truly one of the not-to-be-missed events of the holiday season.

2. City Hall

Where? At Queen and Bay Streets
392-0458 for events hotline
TTC: From Queen Station walk two blocks west along Queen Street, or walk east from Osgoode Station
When? Public access to building weekdays 8 am–4:30 pm
How much? Free
How long? 1 hour for a visit; longer during special events
Extras: Cafeteria, wheelchair and stroller accessible, underground parking

Toronto City Hall, often called New City Hall by Torontonians (Old City Hall is just across Bay Street), vies with the CN Tower as the city's most visible and most often reproduced landmark. Opened in 1965, City Hall's two curved towers encircling a central round pavilion have been likened to a clam shell, and this novel shape appeals to kids, who will come up with their own comparisons. The building fronts onto a

3.6-hectare (9-acre) plaza called **Nathan Phillips Square**, in honour of the mayor who had the foresight to hire Finnish architect Viljo Revell to create an internationally outstanding and daring building that reflected Toronto's growing sophistication.

Visitors are welcome to take a free, self-guided tour of City Hall on weekdays from 8 am to 4:30 pm. The information desk in the foyer will provide a brochure outlining the highlights. Two features not to be overlooked in the main-floor foyer are the sculpture mural "Metropolis," by artist David Partridge, assembled from 100,000 nails, and the scale-model of Toronto, with each

building in place. Also on the main floor is a small shop that sells a few high-quality Toronto souvenirs.

Toronto City Hall achieves Top-10 status for more than its architecture. Over the years Nathan Phillips Square has evolved into a venue for a variety of events and activities that appeal to families, most of which are free and informal. In winter there is the ice skating rink, which draws office workers and kids alike, and the annual Cavalcade of Lights, beginning the last weekend in November and running through the holiday season. The Cavalcade opens with a star-studded skating show and the illumination of over 100,000 lights around City Hall and at nearby locations. Other seasonal events are an ice sculpture competition that draws international artists, a free New Year's Eve party and concert, and an afternoon levee on New Year's Day. Spring brings Bunnymania on Easter weekend, with egg hunts, magic shows, concerts, and a live bunny petting zoo.

Nathan Phillips Square really comes into its own in summer. For families, the best bets are Toronto Kids Tuesdays in July and August, with lunchtime performances by top-notch children's entertainers. Every Wednesday from Victoria Day to Thanksgiving, there is an open-air farmer's market with fresh Ontario produce and baked goods on sale from 10 am to 4 pm, and a free "Sound-sational" concert with performers that range from classical to folk to ethnic traditions. On Canada Day the square hosts another big bash featuring all-day entertainment. On the second weekend in July, the largest outdoor art exhibition in North America takes place in the square, with 500 artists and artisans displaying their work.

While at Nathan Phillips Square, be sure to see the **Henry Moore sculpture** — an untitled piece that has come to be known as "The Archer" — and the graceful **Peace Garden** that commemorates the bombing of Nagasaki and Hiroshima. One last feature of the square that often escapes notice is the great fenced-in playground tucked behind the west wall of City Hall. The playground is reserved for the City Hall daycare centre during certain hours, but the public may use it at other times and on the weekends. Check the playground's public hours, posted on its gate.

3. CN Tower

Where? 301 Front Street West
360-8500
TTC: From Union Station take the SkyWalk to the tower or board the Front-Esplanade bus westbound to John Street; or from King or St. Andrew Station take the King streetcar west to John Street and walk south
When? Observation Decks: 10 am–11 pm daily, open till 12 am in the summer; MindWarp and Q-Zar

operate on more limited hours, for details call 360-8500

How much? To Skypod Observation Decks: $12 for adults, $7 for children 5-12, children under 5 free; additional charges for MindWarp and Q-Zar: $8 for adults, $6.50 for children; discounted combination tickets are available

How long: 1½–2½ hours, depending on line-ups

Extras: Parking rates in this area are usually sky-high; for reasons of cost and traffic, don't even *think* of driving if there is an event at SkyDome

Completed in 1976 and billed as the world's tallest free-standing structure at 553 metres (1815 feet), the CN Tower has become a Toronto icon and is definitely one of the city's premier tourist attractions. As such it is often

67

very crowded; visitors with young children are advised to avoid weekends and peak hours in favour of early-morning or dinner-time tours.

Besides the spectacular bird's-eye view of the city, the tower offers two other attractions at ground level: the **MindWarp** motion simulator ride and **Q-Zar**, a futuristic live-action game. For admission to both of these, children must be at least 106 centimetres (42 inches). Parents should note that these attractions are high-adrenaline, intense, and noisy experiences that some kids (and some adults, for that matter) will find a bit too stimulating.

The thrill of a visit to the CN Tower starts with a 346-metre (1136-foot) elevator ride to the **Skypod's Indoor Observation Deck**. The elevator swooshes up a glassed-in shaft at the speed of a jet plane takeoff and the sensation of watching the city recede below your feet is a heady one. The elevators fill up quickly; try to hop on last so that small people will be able to see. If you feel comfortable doing so, leave your stroller at the elevator entrance (the attendant will keep an eye on it);

you'll likely find it cumbersome, especially on the stairs you must use to reach the Outdoor Observation Level.

On the Indoor Observation Deck, you can watch *To the Top*, an award-winning film on the building of the tower, and have a snack at the **Horizons Bar and Restaurant**, which offers a kids' menu (but don't expect cheap prices in a tourist mecca like the tower). If the kids are really hungry, try to get them to hold out for Tim Horton's or Harvey's in the tower's concourse.

A new interactive exhibit called **Eco Dek** recently opened on the Indoor Observation Level. Eco Dek uses the latest in computer and video technology to persuade visitors to adopt a "greener" lifestyle. Some of the concepts presented may be too sophisticated for kids, but all the high-tech gizmos and doodads are fun to watch.

Your next stop is the **Outdoor Observation Level**, just under the Indoor Observation Level. Here you can stand "on air" and look down at the city through the glass floor under your feet. Kids love tearing around the circular deck to take in the full 360-degree experience. The uppermost level of the Skypod contains the CN Tower's revolving restaurant, where dinner-time prices reach about the same altitude as the top of the tower. If you want to share an elegant dining experience with your (older) children, go at lunch when there is an interesting menu at a fraction of the evening prices. Also, those dining in the revolving restaurant avoid paying the tower admission price.

To go to even greater heights, you'll need to take a second elevator to the Space Deck at 447 metres (1465 feet), for an additional charge of $2.25 (no special kids' rate). Here you will find coin-operated high-power binoculars to help you see as far as Niagara Falls on a clear day, though the view is the same as that a level below, only from a higher perspective and with a surcharge. Given that a trip to the tower is an expensive outing for a family, the cost-conscious might want to skip this extra.

The food court below the tower contains a variety of fast-food outlets. Thankfully, all are served from one cash counter, so visitors don't have to hop from line-up to line-up when ordering different items.

If you are visiting the CN Tower in the summer, try the **Putt-Putt Family Golf Centre**. The children's rate is only $2 for 18 holes of mini-golf and you can pass a pleasant hour here without blowing the budget.

4. Harbourfront ✱

Where? Queen's Quay West from York Street to Spadina Avenue
973-3000
TTC: Take the Harbourfront LRT from Union Station
When? Open daily, hours for events vary
How much? Free access to all sites and to most activities; separate admission rates to some concerts and special events
How long? During good weather, most families can easily fill an afternoon or a whole day at Harbourfront
Extras: Great waterfront strolling, canoe and skate rentals, lots of tasty take-out food in Queen's Quay Terminal for picnicking;

parking at Harbourfront is costly for long visits, less pricey rates can be found in the lots east of the site

Note: As *Toronto with Kids* went to press, funding for Harbourfront's future programming was uncertain. Before you visit, call the information number for details on specific activities.

This 4-hectare (10-acre) complex on Toronto's waterfront offers more activities and attractions than the average family could possibly explore in one day. Harbourfront bills itself as "Toronto's premier centre of community, and cultural, activity" and the hype is justified: every year hundreds of community, cultural, and arts groups sponsor events here.

Harbourfront's hub is **York Quay** (pronounced "key") **Centre**, at the foot of York Street, which contains ten performing and exhibition spaces for year-round activities, plus the country's largest outdoor artificial skating rink (skate rental available) and an elegant two-storey shopping and restaurant complex in the Queen's Quay Terminal Building. For families, one tempting site is the **Kaleidoscope** kids' craft studio on the second floor of the York Quay Centre, which offers free supervised hands-on workshops every weekend, suitable for kids up to age eight. Origami, mask-making, papier mâché, clay modelling, and just about every other craft activity you can think of keep children happily occupied. Older kids can be left unattended by parents at Kaleidoscope; under-sixes should have a parent present.

Also in the York Quay Centre is the **Craft Studio**, where artisans work on glass, metal, textile, and ceramic crafts in full view of the public. Kids are especially fascinated by the glass firing oven and the glass blowing, and will linger to watch the artisans even on the hottest summer day. The creations of these and other top-notch craftspersons are on sale at **Bounty**, the store that adjoins the Craft Studio.

On your way to a snack or a drink at the York Quay Centre's **Water's Edge Café** (liquor licensed), you can take in several art exhibitions at the **York Quay Gallery**, the **Community Gallery**, and the **Photo Passage**. Every Sunday at 2 pm throughout the year there is a free family concert at the café, and if the mood is right, kids will often be dancing in the aisles or on stage with the performers. Harbourfront also hosts the children's music series, **Cushion Concerts**; see page 129 for more information.

The menu at the Water's Edge Café is regular fast-food fare, but during the warm months it's a wonderful spot to have a cold drink on the outside deck and watch the antics of the resident seagull population against the backdrop of Lake Ontario. There is an excellent, though often rather crowded, playground at the southwest corner of the pond. No wading, please; the pond is frequented by hundreds of waterfowl.

Harbourfront's retail centre is the **Queen's Quay Terminal Building**, which houses over 100 stores and several food outlets in an elegantly renovated warehouse which dates from 1926. There are several specialty toy shops in the terminal, including stores devoted to "Sesame Street" merchandise, games, science gizmos, kites, dolls — one shop carries nothing but pigs. The building is also home to the **Premiere Dance Theatre**, Canada's only theatre designated specially for dance; its regular series showcases companies from around the world. In October, the theatre serves as the venue of the **International Authors Festival**, one of the world's largest and most pre-eminent literary events.

Other features of Harbour-front include the **Power Plant**, the city's premier spot for contemporary art; the **Nautical Centre**, which hosts several marine-related events and offers sailing and boating courses; and the **Antiques Market**, on the north side of Queen's Quay, which welcomes browsers every day to its hundreds of stalls.

5. Metropolitan Toronto Zoo ✸

Where? Meadowvale Road north of Sheppard Avenue 392-5900

TTC: From Sheppard Station take the Sheppard East bus, or from Kennedy Station take the Scarborough bus

When? Open year-round, including Christmas Day; hours vary seasonally; opens at 9 or 9:30 am, closes between 4:30 and 7:30 pm

How much? $9.75 for adults, $7 for youths, $5 for children, children 3 and under free

How long? No less than 4 hours

Extras: Stroller and wagon rentals $2, wheelchairs available (no charge), largely stroller and wheelchair accessible, 24 miles of walking trails, Monorail ($2.50) and Zoomobile ($2.50), two gift shops with good selections for young naturalists, picnic area, baby care/nursing area, first-aid station with registered nurse on duty, winter rental of cross-country ski equipment, free use of trails, parking $5 per day

Note: Absolutely no pets are allowed on zoo grounds, including in the parking lot; animals must not be left in parked cars.

The marvellous Metro Zoo is huge — and then some. The six "zoo-geographic regions" are spread out over an area of 287 hectares (710 acres) in a scenic setting in the Rouge River Valley. To explore even half of the regions entails a lot of trekking and if you have younger children in tow, a stroller or wagon (the zoo rents these) is absolutely essential. Don't set out to see the whole zoo in one visit, especially with kids: it just can't be done. Careful planning and a selection of personal must-sees are the keys to a successful visit.

The aim of the Metro Zoo is to show its collection of 5,000 animals in environments that are as natural as possible, while providing both an educational and a recreational experience for visitors. In practice this means that many of the animals are contained in large open areas that give them some room to roam, but often put them at quite a distance from viewers. Small children may find this frustrating, so if your crew is on the young side, concentrate your visit on the indoor pavilions where the inhabitants can be observed more closely. A few of the stars in the geographically designated pavilions include gorillas and chimpanzees (Africa); river otters and venomous snakes — try to catch these at feeding times (Americas); orangutans and monitor lizards (Indo-Malaya); marsupials and nocturnal animals (Australasia); the only Great Indian rhinoceros in Canada (Indian Rhino pavilion); and clouded leopards (Malayan Woods).

Because the zoo is so large, you should pick up a copy of its free *Guide Book and Map* before you start out. It presents five colour-coded trails that criss-cross the site and offers a brief commentary on most of the animals; a handy reference

source for those "What's that, Daddy?" questions.

If you're wondering where all the indigenous Canadian animals are, board the **Monorail** ($2.50) to see them. It's wise to save this part of the visit until you're exhausted from walking; the 40-minute sit-down ride will be all the more enjoyable, although your views of moose, wolves, musk-ox, and such will be fleeting as the train rolls by.

While the zoo's top-notch staff make sure that their animal charges are well fed (check the board near the entrance for the feeding times of various species), the same cannot be said of the human visitors. The only restaurants on the grounds are operated by McDonald's, so if you want to eat, either bring your own supplies or accept your fate as a fast-food captive. After the cost of feeding a large family is added to the admission price (plus parking), you may feel as if you're the one being eaten alive. Warm-weather visitors should pack a Thermos of cold drinks. Kids can get quite parched walking outside between exhibits; there's little shade and water fountains are too few and far between.

In addition to watching the animals feeding, there are other live demonstrations daily: a free flying-bird show and various "meet the keeper" sessions where kids can pose questions to the experts. Camel rides also operate every day except in the worst weather.

West of the entrance there is a special children's area, with a playground, educational displays, pony rides, a petting zoo, and a collection of small animals that the little ones can enjoy up close. If the youngest in your group are getting cranky, this is the ideal spot to let them unwind.

Don't forget to visit the zoo in the winter months, when some of the animals are at their friskiest. All of the animals are on display year-round unless the weather conditions are really fierce. Crowds can be dense during the summer holidays, and an off-season visit is sure to be more pleasant and relaxed.

6. Ontario Place

Where? 955 Lakeshore Boulevard West
314-9900
TTC: From Ossington Station take the Ossington bus south to the Ontario Place entrance
When? Victoria Day weekend through Labour Day, daily 10:30 am–midnight
How much? Free, except during Fireworks Value Days and the Canadian National Exhibition in late August through Labour Day; for $16.95 you can purchase a Play All Day pass (a good deal only if you intend to visit most of the attractions and want to avoid ticket line-ups), which entitles you to free admission to all of the major rides and attractions, except the Molson Amphitheatre and certain Cinesphere shows
How long? No less than 3 hours
Extras: Changerooms and lockers, nursing and baby-changing area, wagon rentals $5 (holds 2 or 3 kids) and stroller rentals $3, largely wheelchair and stroller accessible, parking $9 per day

This 39-hectare (96-acre) amusement complex on the shores of Lake Ontario offers the perfect summer destination for families in search of a not-too-expensive outing that combines lots of fresh air and walking with rides, entertainment, and food.

Built out into the lake on landfill taken from the Bloor-

Danforth subway excavation, Ontario Place, with its geodesic domes and futuristic "pods," is a monument to the government largesse and optimism of the 1960s (the complex opened in 1971). Admission to the grounds is free, which means that you and yours can frolic in the 1.2-hectare (2-acre) Children's Village playground, take in a kids' concert, picnic by the water, or cool off in the Waterplay area for no more than the cost of parking or TTC fare.

Located near the entrance, the **Children's Village** offers over a dozen activities that are oriented to a variety of ages — from toddlers to 12-year-olds. There are huge slides and tunnels, rope climbers, an air bouncer, a ball bath, suspension bridges, and a Tarzan-like cable ride, to name only a few. Parents of very young children will want to keep a close eye on them. In the excitement, little ones may start dashing from activity to activity, and if the playground is crowded you might experience one of those heart-stopping moments when you can't spot your child.

If the kids work up a sweat in the playground, they can cool off in the **Waterplay** area. In addition to the shallow pools, there is an imposing water slide and the **Hydrofuge**, a twisting tunnel slide that spins its riders around in a circular compartment at the bottom before dropping them through a hole into the pool.

The slide has a 114-centimetre (45-inch) height minimum; the Hydrofuge is limited to kids over 122 centimetres (48 inches). Both water slides have admission fees of $3. The area is well monitored by trained lifeguards.

Just west of the Waterplay area is the **Children's Festival Stage**; throughout the main season, it is the site of several free shows daily featuring well-known children's performers and figures like Babar the Elephant, Polkaroo, and Big Bird. These productions provide excellent family entertainment and there's always lots of audience participation.

The other major free attractions for kids are the **LEGO Pod** and the **Nintendo Power Pod**, located in the tower-like pod structures attached by a walkway to **Cinesphere**, the dome-shaped movie theatre. The LEGO display has mind-blowing motorized LEGO constructions made from over a quarter of a million LEGO pieces, along with ample work tables where kids of all ages can make their own LEGO and DUPLO assemblages. The Nintendo Power Pod has

scores of the video games on monitors and the kids can run wild trying all of their favourites.

Cinesphere houses a six-storey-high screen for IMAX films that give the giddy sensation of being right in the action. There can be a long line-up, but if the kids can tolerate the wait it's usually worth it. You may want to ask at the box office if the film has any scenes that might frighten young children; the impact of seeing these on such a large screen can be overwhelming. Cinesphere shows are $6 for adults and $3 for children 12 and under.

At the Ontario Place entrance you will find the **HMCS *Haida*** permanently at anchor. This Canadian warship gives a fascinating glimpse of shipboard life, complete with displays of World War II artifacts. There is a small additional charge to visit the ship.

The older kids in your group will likely want to try out some of Ontario Place's paying attractions: the **SeaTrek** submarine simulator, the **Laser Fantasy** 3-D rock 'n' roll light show, the **Wilderness Adventure** flume

77

ride, and **MegaMaze**, a walk-through six-maze puzzle. All cost under $5 to visit. Note that all of these attractions carry warnings that they might be risky for people with certain medical conditions. The laser show is next to the Nintendo Power Pod; all other attractions are located on the West Island, which is quite a hike from the Children's Village. You may choose to take the free shuttle boat to the West Island or back. Ask a park staffer for directions to the docks.

There are a variety of food outlets on the Ontario Place grounds. Prices tend to be reasonable overall, but there are no bargains and no great cuisine either. If you want to sit on a restaurant terrace overlooking the water, try an off-peak hour; these tables fill up fast. If you head over to the Island Club on the West Island, you might enjoy a free musical show with your meal. Or bring a picnic and dine by the waterfront.

The 16,000-seat **Molson Amphitheatre** is the venue for daily evening and weekend performances by top Canadian and international stars throughout the summer. Ticket prices vary and seats must generally be booked in advance. There are also unreserved lawn spaces for 7000 people. Call Ontario Place for a show schedule and ticket prices.

7. Ontario Science Centre ✱

Where? 770 Don Mills Road 696-3127

TTC: From Pape Station take the Don Mills bus, or from Eglinton Station take the Eglinton East bus

When? 10 am–6 pm daily (closed Christmas Day)

How much? $7.50 for adults, $5.50 for youths (11–17 years), $3 for children (5–10 years) and seniors, children under 5 free, $17 for family of 2 adults and children under 18, admission by donation Wednesdays after 4 pm

How long? No less than 3 hours

Extras: Excellent gift shop emphasizing science-related toys and learning materials for all ages, wheelchair and stroller accessible, strollers available, diaper-changing tables in all washrooms, parking $4 per day

The Ontario Science Centre is a playground of science and technology set in a cascading series of interconnected structures that tumble dramatically into the Don River Valley. The buildings are linked by long ramps and escalators that kids love to run along or ride. If you're looking for an indoor outing that still provides lots of exercise, the Science Centre will fit the bill.

With a mission to promote an awareness of science and technology, the Science Centre has over 650 exhibits relating to astronomy, geology, biology, ecology, chemistry, physics, communications, and transportation. It has taken interactive learning to the limit and most of the displays involve buttons to push, handles to pull, touch-activated computer screens, and a whole array of devices that enthral children. If there is any downside, it's that kids can be so caught up in

manipulating the technology of the exhibits that they completely overlook what they're supposed to be learning from them. Another potential problem is that most of the exhibits require reading skills for a full appreciation. While prereaders will still have a great time here, don't expect them to understand what they're seeing without a lot of input from you. Parents who are "science-challenged" may wish they'd paid more attention during their high-school physics class.

Among the centre's many worthwhile features are the daily demonstrations in the exhibit areas. The times for these are posted as you descend the escalator to Level C. There the **Laser show**, performed several times a day, is a favourite where kids can watch a laser beam cut through Plexiglas, or see how it's used in delicate eye surgery. On the same level, there's **Starlab**, a mini-planetarium where you can experience travel through the solar system. On Level D, kids line up again and again to have their hair stand on end in the **Electricity demonstration**.

An exhibit that visitors of all ages can enjoy is the **Tropical Rainforest** in the Living Earth exhibition on Level D. Constructed in 1993, this area also houses a spooky Ontario limestone cave, which youngsters can walk through, and tanks that display the live ecosystems of a tropical coral reef and the Bay of Fundy. The Tropical Rainforest is a "body-in" exhibit containing over 350 species of vegetation, growing and decaying just as they would in the wild. The atmosphere is hot and steamy with 90 percent humidity, and those shrill notes you hear are coming from over 100 poison dart-frogs — don't worry, they're in glass cages. Exhibit designers have even made the path through the rainforest wide enough for baby strollers.

Another surefire hit is the **Sport exhibit** on Level C. There's lots of opportunity here to make the muscles move: a rock-climbing wall, wheelchair-racing platform, pitching cage, and balance beam, to name only a few. There's also a thrilling simulated ride on a racing bobsled for your would-be daredevils. Be prepared to have trouble pulling the kids away from this exhibit: you may have to resort to reminders of the Tim Horton Donuts concession on the entrance level.

The Science Centre operates many interactive family work-shops on weekends and hosts a variety of special events throughout the year. There are programs and day camps for kids during Christmas, March Break, and the summer; call the centre for information and for a schedule of upcoming events.

8. Paramount Canada's Wonderland

Where? 9580 Jane Street at Highway 400 and Major Mackenzie Drive
905-832-7000
1-800-363-1990

Transit: Wonderland Express GO buses run regularly from York Mills and Yorkdale Stations

When? Weekends only in May, open daily from Victoria Day weekend to Labour Day, weekends only from Labour Day to Thanksgiving Sunday; admission from 10 am to variable closing times between 6 pm and 10 pm, depending on the time of year

How much? $17.95 for grounds admission only (no rides or shows), $28.95 for pay-one-price passport (ages 7–59), $14.95 for

children 3–6 or under 122 centimetres (48 inches) and seniors, children 2 and under free

Note: If you intend to make more than one visit, you may pay less by buying a Family Season Pass for $169.95 for four people, $42.50 for each additional family member

How long? A full day

Extras: Infant-care areas, rental strollers, wheelchairs available (deposit required), lost child and first-aid services, bank machines, credit cards accepted, pet kennels (fee), parking $6.50 per day

This 121-hectare (300-acre) theme park on the northern fringe of Metro is an irresistible magnet for many families, and it certainly offers a thrill a minute. But if you go, be prepared to spend, spend, spend for all that fun, fun, fun. A family of four will be hard pressed to get out of the park for less than $150 if they purchase any food or souvenirs, and the pervasive commercialism of Wonderland makes it unlikely that you'll be able to resist the kids' entreaties to buy, buy, buy.

So what do you get for these big bucks? By its own count, Wonderland houses over 140 attractions, including 50 rides, a 4-hectare (10-acre) water park, and several live shows. It's best known for its roller coasters, the greatest variety in one spot in North America. Scattered throughout the park are six huge coaster rides, including **Vortex**, Canada's only suspended roller coaster, **Skyrider**, a stand-up looping coaster, and **The Bat**, a genuinely terrifying-looking backwards and forwards looping whirl. As with all the rides at Wonderland, the coasters' entrance ways are marked with size and medical restrictions for riders. Also offered are brief descriptions of the rides, so that thrill-seekers will have an idea of what they're in for.

Many of the full-scale rides at Wonderland are not suitable for young children, but there are the separate **Kid's Kingdom** and **Hanna-Barbera Land** that feature tamer thrills, including a small wooden roller coaster and a large playground. If your kids are under five, you'd be well advised to bring a stroller or wagon, as there's a lot of walking involved. On hot summer days, the site offers little shade, so remember to bring sunscreen, hats, perhaps even a parasol, and to pack a Thermos of cold drinks.

Live shows range from ice skating to high-diving to all-singing, all-dancing revues. These are slickly produced and entertaining, and give fun-stressed parents a chance to take a break. The recent sale of the park to Paramount Pictures Inc. means that many of the shows are tied to their films, like *Star Trek* and *Days of Thunder*. Similarly, the shops are filled with "exclusive movie merchandise," and costumed characters, among them Fred Flintstone, Yogi Bear, and assorted Klingons and Vulcans, roam the grounds. The **Kingswood Theatre** presents large concerts with big-name international headliners; ticket prices are not included in Wonderland admission.

The food, like everything else at Wonderland, is expensive and the selection doesn't venture beyond the fast-food category. The park has a policy of asking its guests not to bring in their own food — there are no designated picnic areas within the grounds — but unless you are willing to pay $3.50 for an ice cream bar or a hot dog, you'll discreetly disregard this suggestion.

Overall, Wonderland is maintained to an almost surgical level of cleanliness — no grotty midway atmosphere here — and there are lots of washrooms throughout the park. If you're ready to spend the cash, a day at Canada's Wonderland will be action packed, especially for preteens and teenagers who can take full advantage of those stomach-churning rides. But if your kids are very young, or if your budget is not elastic, consider visiting Ontario Place or catching rides at the more tranquil Centreville amusement park on the Toronto Islands.

9. Royal Ontario Museum ★

Where? 100 Queen's Park
586-8000 24-hour recording
586-5549 main switchboard
TTC: Right beside Museum Station
When? From Labour Day to Victoria Day open daily; Tuesdays 10 am–8 pm, Wednesdays–Saturdays 10 am–6 pm, Sundays 11 am–6 pm; from Victoria

Day to Labour Day open daily 10 am–6 pm, Tuesdays 10 am–8 pm

How much? $7 for adults, $4 for students, $3.50 for children 5–14 years, $15 for a family (2 adults and up to 4 children), free admission for all on Tuesdays after 4:30 pm

How long? 4 hours

Extras: Stroller rental $1, wheelchairs available (no charge), wheelchair accessible, coat check $1, lockers 50¢, cafeteria

There is no place as magical or as packed with stuff to learn about, wonder over, and just plain enjoy than the venerable Royal Ontario Museum: four floors crammed with centuries — even millennia — of artifacts, treasures, and discoveries from around the globe.

The ROM is immense and somewhat confusing to navigate (its signage is a little *too* tasteful for museum-dazed parents to easily find what they're looking for). A museum plan is indispensable; be sure to ask for one when you pay your admission. The following exhibits are recommended as guaranteed kid-pleasers.

The **S.R. Perren Gem and**

Gold Room (first floor) has the air of a king's treasury, with hundreds of precious stones sparkling and glinting in a truly dazzling display.

The **Dinosaurs Gallery** (second floor), with over a dozen fully assembled skeletons and numerous other displays, will satisfy even the most jaded dino-lover.

The **Bat Cave** (second floor) is a replica of a Jamaican cave with over 4000 stuffed and mounted examples of the creatures. My kids have visited this exhibit at least 20 times, but they still find it wonderfully creepy to walk through the life-like cave with its recorded twitterings and swooping sounds. (Very young children might find this exhibit frighteningly realistic.)

The **Ancient Egypt Exhibit**

(third floor) never fails to intrigue with its example of an intact Egyptian mummy in its case.

Arms and Armour (third floor) is usually a big hit with boys, who are just as fascinated by medieval techniques of warfare as they are by the high-tech arsenal of TV superheroes.

Other areas where the museum excels in its collections are the **Gallery of Birds**, where kids can play with a "build-a-bird" computer program; **Reptiles** (lots of snakes); and its **T.T. Tsui Gallery of Chinese Art**, which includes a Ming Tomb whose massive stone figures are impressive for youngsters to walk among.

For kids, the one frustration of museum visiting is the No Touch policy, but this rule is made to be broken at the ROM's **Discovery Centre** (floor 2B, take the small main-floor elevator beside the Eaton Court). Here children can handle samples from every category of the museum's collections. All of the specimens and artifacts in the centre are real and they are arranged in displays that simulate how curatorial staff actually work.

The Discovery Centre is chock-a-block with neat stuff like dinosaur bones, snakes preserved in jars, bugs of every description, and skeletons. There are microscopes and slides, large magnifying lenses, and other tools of the museum trade, all designed to be used by young visitors. Stacks of clearly marked boxes full of specimens of everything from textiles to pottery shards to fossils are meant to be removed and taken to the study tables, where kids can investigate them up close and answer some challenging quizzes.

The Discovery Centre is restricted to children aged six to twelve; six- to nine-year-olds must have a supervising adult with them, while older kids can spend an hour in the centre alone. If you have a younger child, the staff will give you boxes of items to look through with your child in the area just outside the centre. The centre is staffed by several helpful assistants who relish the chance to answer questions and demonstrate the displays. The Discovery Centre is open from 1 to 5 pm on weekends (extended hours during the

Christmas and March Breaks); during the week it is primarily intended for school groups, but there is some public access. Call first if you want to visit the centre on a weekday.

The museum offers family programming two Sundays per month, usually the first and last. These free activities include hands-on crafts and special demonstrations of music, dance, or storytelling by various community groups, and they are thematically tied to an ongoing exhibit or an aspect of the museum's collections. No preregistration is needed and events usually run from 12 pm to 4 pm.

The ROM's Saturday Morning Clubs and Summer Clubs are extremely popular with local families. These programs run for several weeks and are restricted to kids aged six to fourteen. They run the gamut from archaeology to zoology. Preregistration is essential and a fee is charged.

Adjoining the ROM is the **McLaughlin Planetarium**, which mounts star and laser shows at set hours throughout the day. Admission to these shows is extra, but there is a discount if you are visiting the planetarium on the same day as the museum. Planetarium staff usually advise against taking very young children into a show where the darkness and sound effects could be distressing, and each show comes with a specific age recommendation. Call 586-5736

for a description of the current shows and their suitability for your kids. Admission to the planetarium's exhibit area is included with your ROM admission and you can enter the planetarium through the first floor of the museum.

The **George R. Gardiner Museum of Ceramic Art**, across the street from the ROM, holds limited appeal for most kids with its displays of fine porcelain, china, and other fragile treasures. However, it's worth visiting the Gardiner during the Christmas season to see its knockout display of designer-decorated Christmas trees, each extravagantly and imaginatively decked out in a theme from a familiar children's story or folk tale.

Admission to the Gardiner is included with ROM entry.

10. Toronto Islands ✱

When the noise and bustle of the city start to wear thin, families should head for the Toronto Islands, which constitute a unique parkland only a ten-minute ferry ride from the harbour. Although the islands attract thousands of visitors on hot summer weekends, once you get off the ferry and walk for a few minutes, you'll find an uncrowded oasis full of amenities and attractions for everyone. Plan to make your islands visit last the better part of a day, to take in all of the activities, and allow some time for stretching out on the grass and watching the clouds go by.

There are lots of ways to see the islands besides walking. You can rent bicycles, including tandems, two-seaters, and four-seaters; the latter are great for two adults and a couple of young kids who get to sit up front and be wheeled about like little potentates. There are also boat rentals (canoes, rowboats, and paddleboats) that allow you to play *voyageur* in the lagoons and observe the colonies of birds that nest there. If you want to get around on the cheap and let someone else do the driving, board the free trackless train; it makes a circuit every 15 minutes and can be picked up at various stations along the route.

A day at the islands would be incomplete without a picnic, and there are tables and barbecues in many locations. Bring your own feast and if you would like, supplement it with snacks from the six concessions, which offer the usual range of fast food.

Centre Island

Centre Island, the main destination for most islands visitors, is actually several islands joined by footbridges and lagoons. Its views of the city are nothing short of breathtaking, but the chief attraction for kids is **Centreville** (head east from the ferry docks), a small privately operated amusement park with rides, games, snackbars, and the adjacent **Far Enough Farm** with its modest collection of farm animals. If your kids want to try most of the rides, it's economical to buy an all-day pass and just let them go to it. One delightful feature is the enchanting turn-of-the-century carousel, with its ornate carved animals and vigorous oompah music. There are also bumper cars, a flume ride, a miniature locomotive, swan boats, and numerous other rides and games.

There are two full playgrounds on Centre Island and many other pieces of play equipment scattered around the parkland, along with two wading pools. The beach on the north side near the pier is a comfortable place for kids to paddle, as any waves from the lake are tamed by the breakwater, but swimming is not usually recommended owing to pollution.

When? Centreville operates from Victoria Day weekend to Labour Day; before July 1, 10:30 am–6 pm weekdays, 10:30 am–8 pm weekends; after July 1, 10:30 am–8 pm
How much? All-day passes: $46.50 for a family (4 people, at least 1 adult), $15 for kids over 122 centimetres (48 inches), $10 for kids under 122 centimetres (48 inches); most rides charge at least 2 tickets at 90¢ each
Extras: Bicycle rentals per hour: $5 for a regular, $9 for a tandem, $15 for a 2-seater (2 adults, 1 small child), $22 for a 4-seater (2 adults, 2 kids); deposit and ID required. Boat rentals per hour: $12 for canoes and rowboats, $15 for paddleboats; deposit and ID required. Changerooms, washrooms, first-aid station, lost children station, marina, 2 licensed restaurants.

Wards Island

Toronto prides itself on being a city of neighbourhoods, but of all the diverse communities Toronto has to offer, the small settlement (250 homes) on Wards Island is surely the most unusual. With its random mix of tumbledown cottages and spiffy renos lining narrow, overgrown lanes, Wards attracts artists who love to paint its picturesque views. The absence of cars makes the hamlet on Wards Island feel like a throwback to a much earlier, more innocent time. In fact, Wards is said to be the only carless community in Canada.

When you leave the ferry head west towards the numbered streets and stroll among the cottages. You will find the residents are welcoming — they're used to voyeurs from "the mainland" passing through — and if it's not during school hours, there will be lots of kids playing outside or heading towards the beach.

After you've done the "house tour," you should easily find Lakeshore Avenue, which will lead you to Wards Island's fairly secluded beaches and to the boardwalk. The boardwalk extends to Centre Island, finishing up not far from the bicycle rental kiosk and the 160-metre (520-foot) pier that juts into Lake Ontario. The boardwalk is ideal for baby strollers and bicycles; the wall of flowering vegetation (lilacs, primroses, raspberry bushes) offers a rare sense of seclusion if you are lucky to be there during a non-peak time. If you duck through one of the numerous passages that intersect the vegetation, you'll stumble upon North America's only Frisbee "golf course," so pack your disc and see if you can beat the kids at this offbeat sport.

Hanlan's Point

This is the third islands destination, and like Wards it offers a less hectic and less commercialized outing, with the bonus of views of the takeoffs and landings at the Toronto City Centre Airport and of Toronto's oldest lighthouse. Hanlan's has good beaches — some are popular with Toronto's gay community — and tennis courts. There is fishing for trout and bass at the pond near the **Gibraltar Point Lighthouse** (bring your own gear). The lighthouse was built in 1809 and is rumoured to be haunted by the ghost of the first lighthouse keeper, who was murdered by some troops from Fort York for refusing to share his whiskey with them. The kids might also be interested in taking a look at the **Island Science School**, close by the lighthouse; originally established in 1888 as a one-room school for islands residents, it was destroyed by fire in 1905. Rebuilt and expanded over the next 30 years to a four-room school, it peaked at 587 students in 1954. In 1960 it was converted to a natural science school, which is attended by mainland students for a week at a time.

If you'd like to make a day of walking between the three islands, make note of the following distances: from Wards Island docks to Hanlan's Point docks is 5 kilometres (3 miles); Wards Island to Centre Island docks is 2.5 kilometres (1.5 miles); Hanlan's Point to Centre Island docks is 3.75 kilometres (2.3 miles).

Toronto Islands Ferries

Where? Foot of Bay Street
392-8193
TTC: From Union Station take the Harbourfront LRT
How much? All ferries (return trip): $3 for adults, $1.50 for students (under 18) and seniors, $1 for children 2–12 years, children under 2 free

Riding the ferry to Toronto Islands is one of the most pleasant experiences the city has to offer, and kids never seem to tire of it. The boats are quaint, the views panoramic, and passengers enjoy the sensation of getting away from it all as the city recedes behind the ferry's wake and the seagulls wheel above.

The ferry docks are located at the foot of Bay Street, just west of the Westin Harbour Castle hotel. In warm weather you'll be able to spot them easily from the throng of hot dog and ice cream vendors attracted here by the heavy pedestrian traffic. If you are driving to the docks, the cheapest parking is west of the hotel, along Queen's Quay, about a ten-minute walk from the ferry.

At the docks there are washrooms, telephones, and a limited snackbar. The ferries have washrooms and are fully equipped with life-saving equipment. Bicycles are permitted on the ferries, except to and from Centre Island on weekends and holidays in the summer. During special events or on hot summer weekends the boats to Centre Island can become very crowded and visitors with strollers might consider riding to Hanlan's or Wards and enjoying the walk to Centre Island (these walks would likely be too long for young children on foot).

There are four regular vessels that make the ten-minute run to the islands. The *William Inglis*, built in 1935, is a 30-metre (99-foot) diesel-powered boat, named after a prominent businessman. The *Sam McBride*, built in 1939, is named after a popular mayor. The *Thomas Rennie*, built in 1951, is named after a longtime harbour commissioner. If you are going to Wards or Hanlan's, sometimes an open-air ride can be had on the *Ongiara*, a freight boat that offers a bit more of a thrill for young sailors.

Ferry Schedule

SUMMER SCHEDULE:
Victoria Day to Labour Day

Weekdays:

To Centre Island:
Generally ferries depart every half-hour on the hour from 8 am to 11 pm; service is increased to every 15 minutes if crowds are large

To Wards Island:
Departures every half-hour to 45 minutes during the morning and afternoon rush hours; during the rest of the day service runs every hour from 8:45 am to 2:45 pm

To Hanlan's Point:
Departures every half-hour on the hour from 9 am to 10 pm

Weekends:

To Centre Island: Departures every half-hour from 8 am to 10:30 am; then every 15 minutes to 6:30 pm; every half-hour from 6:30 pm to 11:30 pm

To Wards Island: Departures every 45 minutes 8 am to 11 am; then every 30 minutes until 7 pm; every 45 minutes 7 pm to 11:30 pm

To Hanlan's Point:
Departures every 45 minutes from 8 am to 10:15 am; then every 30 minutes until 6:15 pm; every 45 minutes until 10:45 pm

Note: Times are subject to change. Call 392-8193 to confirm schedule or to obtain hours of operation during the other seasons. The Centre Island ferries operate only in the summer.

5: In days of old

Although by the standards of European or Asian cities Toronto is a mere infant of only 161 years, it does have a rich trove of historic sites, buildings, and museums that can provide the occasion for children to learn about the city's and the country's past, while being amply entertained at the same time. Whether it's Toronto's marine and trading history at the Marine Museum of Upper Canada, the lifestyles of some of its most illustrious citizens at the Toronto Historical Board's restored homes, or the daily life of early settlers at Black Creek Pioneer Village, young people can experience it all at Toronto's many history-related attractions.

Bata Shoe Museum ✱

Where? 327 Bloor Street West
979-7799
TTC: Opposite
St. George Station
When? Tuesdays,
Wednesdays, Fridays, and
Saturdays 10 am–5 pm;
Thursdays 10 am–8 pm;
Sundays 12–5 pm; closed
Mondays
How much? $6 for adults, $2
for children 5–14 years,
$12 for a family, children
under 5 free
How long: 1½ hours

This unique museum cheerfully boasts that it offers "a look at history from below the knees," and with a collection of over 10,000 shoes to draw on for its exhibits, the Bata Shoe Museum delivers on this promise. Founded by Sonia Bata of the internationally successful Bata Shoe Company, and housed in a stunning new building near the University of Toronto, the museum is best suited to the interests of fashion-conscious preteens and teens who will be intrigued by the wide-ranging array of footwear through the centuries and across continents.

Here you'll find everything from hand-embroidered Lapp reindeer-skin boots to silver Turkish wedding stilt-sandals

to four-inch-spiked chestnut-crushing boots used in the early shoe-making trade. Kids are sure to be appalled by the two-inch-long embroidered slippers worn by bound-footed Chinese noblewomen, while Elton John's eight-inch platform boots will appeal to young rockers. The inclusion of contemporary shoe fads like brand-name runners and Doc Martens might help clothes-crazy kids take a long view of the dictates of fashion.

Black Creek ✱ Pioneer Village

Where? 1000 Murray Ross Parkway (Jane Street and Steeles Avenue)
736-1733
TTC: From Jane Station take the Jane bus, or from Finch Station take the Finch bus west to Jane Street
When? The village is closed from January 1 to May 1; from May 1 to December 31 it is open daily (except Christmas Day) from 10 am to 5 pm
How much? $7.50 for adults, $5 for seniors and students, $3.25 for children 5–14, children under 5 free

How long? At least 3 hours

Extras: Dining room with historic atmosphere, horse-drawn wagon rides, sleigh rides, limited access to some buildings for wheelchairs and strollers, free parking

A re-creation of a rural Upper Canadian community of the 1860s, Black Creek Pioneer Village is a lively site with about three dozen buildings that include homes, work-shops, meeting halls, a school, a church, and barns. The village was built around the homestead of a Pennsylvania German settler named Daniel Stong, and his barns and two homes are original to the site. All of the other buildings were moved from their first locations to Black Creek. Today the village bustles with all of the daily activities that went on in such a settlement over 130 years ago.

For visitors with kids, the best feature of the village is its combination of "living history" with lots of fresh air. It takes at least three hours to see everything, which means a good walk in a postcard-pretty spot, complete with a millpond, grazing sheep, and apple orchards. Gardens scattered throughout the village are planted and cultivated as they would have been in the mid-19th century. There are several demonstrations of pioneer crafts by costumed staff — tinsmithing, weaving, clock-making, printing, and broom-making, to name only a few — plus a working grist mill that sells bags of its wholesome flour.

Black Creek Pioneer Village celebrates the seasons with numerous festivals and events. There are spring and fall fairs, with Victorian kids' games and goings-on, and in the summer a theatre company presents vignettes of pioneer life. Halloween is full of games and mischief, and Christmas sees the entire village decked out in early-Canadian finery with lots of Yule yummies on offer, and a resident Santa. One very special event is the Christmas by Lamplight evenings, when the village is open in the evening and lit by the romantic glow of lamp and candlelight (these evenings must be prebooked).

South from the village is a 2-kilometre (1.25-mile) walk through **Black Creek Ravine** that leads to **Northwood Park** at Sheppard and Seeley Avenues. This stretch along Black Creek was a Huron settlement over 3000 years ago; it underwent archaeological excavation in the 1940s and '50s. A paved trail/bicycle path passes through woodland areas rich in wildlife and an abundance of plant varieties. Just below Finch Avenue there is a picnic area, with drinking fountains and washrooms.

Colborne Lodge

Where? High Park, south end, on Colborne Lodge Drive
392-6916
TTC: From High Park Station walk 15 minutes through the park, or take the Humber streetcar to Colborne Lodge Drive
When? From April through December open Tuesdays–Fridays 9:30 am–5 pm; Saturdays and Sundays

12–5 pm; from January through March open Saturdays, Sundays, and holidays 12–5 pm
How much? $3.50 for adults, $2.75 for students, $2.50 for children
How long: 1 hour
Extras: A charming Dickensian Christmas celebration from late November to January 6; all of High Park to explore after your Colborne Lodge visit

Colborne Lodge was the home of architect and engineer John Howard and his wife, Jemima, and is named after Howard's patron, Sir John Colborne, Lieutenant-Governor of Upper Canada from 1828 to 1836. This Regency picturesque-style villa was situated originally on 65 hectares (160 acres) of land that Howard called High Park, territory he donated to the City of Toronto on his death.

The house is restored to the style of 1870 and contains many of the Howards' original belongings. Several of the paintings are by Howard and provide a fascinating glimpse of the city over 100 years ago, when the lodge's occupants enjoyed an unobstructed view down to the lake.

Costumed guides provide tours of the house and willingly answer kids' questions on any subject. Most children are enthralled by the original bathroom and "water closet" on the main floor. Among the first indoor facilities in Toronto, they were equipped with the latest innovations — flush toilets and running water. The commodious and comfortable-looking tub appears especially inviting, but it had no drain and was emptied by servants using buckets.

Upstairs are two children's bedrooms used by the Howards' nieces (they had no children themselves) that show how even the well-to-do were accustomed to living in much more constricted spaces than we are used to today.

The two kitchens, summer upstairs and winter downstairs, are crammed full of period implements and there are often cookies on hand, baked by the lodge's staff. Guessing games about what various tools are and how they work help to involve kids in imagining life before microwaves and washing machines.

The Howards' gravesite is located on the other side of Colborne Lodge Road, north of the house. Designed by Howard himself — whose will stipulated that the couple's grave would be maintained forever by the city — the monument is surrounded by a section of fence from St. Paul's Cathedral in London, England, designed by the famous architect Christopher Wren.

Enoch Turner Schoolhouse

Where? 106 Trinity Street 863-0010
TTC: Take the King streetcar to Trinity Street, one stop east of Parliament Street
When? 10 am–4:30 pm weekdays
How much? Free, but call first to be sure that the schoolhouse has not been prebooked by a group
How long? ½ hour
Extras: Free parking on Power Street, courtesy of Black & McDonald Ltd

This charming Victorian schoolhouse is the site of Toronto's first public school, the gift of brewer Enoch Turner to the city's poor children, who were unable to afford private education. Opened in 1849, the school originally held 240 pupils — with desks for only one-third! The West Hall extension, completed in 1869, was used for over 100 years as a Sunday school.

Kids are sure to be intrigued by the 19th-century schoolroom, complete with rulers for knuckle-rapping and an old stove that probably did little to thaw frozen fingers during Toronto's frigid winters. Guides happily answer children's questions about early schooling and kids can try out the old-fashioned desks and benches. There's lots of scope for letting youngsters use their imaginations to speculate on what their lives would have been like as pupils here almost 150 years ago.

Torontonians should be grateful that the schoolhouse was rescued from its date with the wrecker's ball in the 1960s to be restored as one of North America's best educational museums and as a vibrant community centre. If you have a few extra minutes, take a peek at nearby **Little Trinity Church**, which is the city's oldest surviving church (1845)

and a modest architectural gem. There is a small playground behind the church.

Fort York ✱

Where? Garrison Road, off Fleet Street, between Bathurst and Strachan Streets
392-6907
TTC: Take the Bathurst streetcar to the Exhibition Place loop
When? Open in winter Tuesdays–Fridays 9:30 am–4 pm; Saturdays, Sundays, and holidays 10 am–5 pm; open daily in summer 9:30 am–5 pm
How much? $5 for adults, $3.25 for seniors and youths 13–18, $3 for children 6–12, children under 6 free
How long? 1–2 hours
Extras: Small snackbar, souvenir shop, limited stroller and wheelchair accessibility for some buildings, free parking, history-based programs for kids on Sundays during the summer

The fortified walls of Fort York surround Canada's largest collection of original War of 1812 buildings. A garrison was first established at this site in 1793 by Lieutenant-Governor John Graves Simcoe, who feared imminent naval attack by the United States (at that time the fort was located close to the shoreline of Lake Ontario, now hundreds of metres south, thanks to landfill operations).

These tensions eventually eased and the colony's main defences were moved to Kingston, Ontario, while a small garrison remained at York.

In 1807, Anglo-American relations deteriorated again and Major-General Isaac Brock strengthened Fort York in 1811. The Americans invaded in April 1813, occupying the town of York and burning the government buildings. In August 1814, a rebuilt Fort York was strong enough to repel an American squadron that attempted to take control of Toronto Bay.

Fort York was used by first the British and then the Canadian army until the 1930s. In 1909, the fort was purchased by the City of Toronto, and it opened as a historical site in 1934. Today it is operated by the Toronto Historical Board.

There are several daily tours of the fort by costumed interpreters who give visitors the flavour of everyday life in this quite primitive military setting. Kids are amazed to hear that the soldiers' 1815 barracks housed 100 people: soldiers, their wives, and their children, often sleeping five or six to a bunk. Soldiers were issued a cloth that they used to wash their hands, face, and feet (!) daily; baths were but a twice-annual event.

The officers enjoyed a far more comfortable, even gracious style of life in their barracks and mess. This 1815 brick

building contains a working kitchen that is usually staffed by a cook/interpreter who cheerfully dispenses freshly baked cakes and other treats made from authentic recipes.

Two of the other buildings house displays of military artifacts and local history. After you've visited all the buildings, a walk along the fortified walls with their cannon emplacements rounds out the tour and provides some photogenic views of the fort's humble wooden structures set against the futuristic backdrop of SkyDome and the CN Tower. Your kids might enjoy staging some mock-battle scenes of their own in the fort's large open parade ground.

Gibson House

Where? 5172 Yonge Street
395-7432
TTC: From North York
Centre Station walk north
on Yonge Street
When? Tuesdays–Fridays
9:30 am–5 pm, weekends
and holidays 12–5 pm
How much? $2.50 for adults,
$1.50 for children, $6 for a
family
How long? 1 hour

Although civic boosters in North York take greatest pride in the glass office and condo towers that line this stretch of north Yonge Street, one of the area's real gems dates from the 1850s. Gibson House, the ten-room Georgian-style mansion of surveyor David Gibson, Eliza Gibson, and their family of seven children, now operates as a museum with monthly special events that offer young visitors insight into 19th-century life, whether it's an exhibit of Victorian toys and games or a demonstration of cures and concoctions based on herbs from the family's garden. During school holiday periods in the summer, March, and December, the staff conduct hands-on activity programs for children (preregistration required).

Holocaust Education and Memorial Centre

Where? 4600 Bathurst
Street, between Sheppard
and Finch Avenues
635-2883
TTC: Take the Bathurst bus;
ask to be let off at the Jewish
Community Centre and

walk north to the Lipa
Green Building
When? Tuesdays and
Thursdays 1–4:30 pm,
Sundays 11 am–4:30 pm
How much? Free
How long? 1 hour

Dedicated to the memory of the
millions of Jews persecuted and
killed during the Holocaust and
to promote a deeper understanding of this tragic episode
in history, the centre presents a
panorama of Jewish life in
pre-Nazi Europe: a continuous
slide presentation entitled
"Images of the Holocaust" and
an audio-visual documentary.

At a time when so many
parents and educators bemoan
the younger generation's
ignorance of recent history, a
visit to the solemn memorial
centre could be a useful tool to
open discussions with your kids
on a range of important events
and issues.

Mackenzie House

Where? 82 Bond Street
392-6915
TTC: From Dundas Station
walk two blocks east to
Bond Street

When? Saturdays and
Sundays 12–5 pm, weekday
schedule varies through the
year; call to confirm hours
How much? $3.50 for adults,
$2.75 for youths 13–18, $2.50
for children 4–12
How long? 1 hour

Toronto's first mayor and the
leader of the 1837 Upper
Canada Rebellion, William
Lyon Mackenzie, made his home
here between 1859 and 1861.

Like Toronto's other historical
houses, it has period furnishings, and visitors are wel-
comed with treats from the
kitchen. The house's unique
feature is the 19th-century
printing press used by Mac-

kenzie to churn out his newspaper, *The Colonial Advocate*. Today the press is operated (at selected times) by a printer who demonstrates its workings for visitors and often allows kids to print their own sheets as special take-home souvenirs.

Marine Museum of Upper Canada

Where? Exhibition Place (Canadian National Exhibition grounds) 392-1765
TTC: Take the Bathurst streetcar to Exhibition Place
When? Tuesdays–Fridays 9:30 am–5 pm, weekends 12–5 pm
How much? $3.50 for adults, $2.75 for students and seniors, $2.50 for children
How long? 1–2 hours
Extras: Free parking outside Exhibition Place (though the lot fills up quickly during major events at the CNE grounds), souvenir shop with lots of nautical-themed toys and gifts

This unassuming two-storey museum, located in the 1841 Stanley Barracks (originally part of the New Fort that replaced Fort York), is an impressive treasury of information about Toronto Harbour and its role in the city's and the nation's development.

From the birch-bark canoes of the fur trade to the modern steamships of today, the museum contains a wealth of

ship models, along with other marine-related displays like gleaming steam whistles and bells, and early scuba and telecommunications equipment. Kids can tap out the Morse code on a wireless operator's set and wonder at the strange relics retrieved over the years by divers in Toronto Harbour.

On the grounds of the museum are a 1942 steam locomotive and the *Ned Hanlan*, a steam tugboat launched in 1932, which visitors can board from May through October.

Metropolitan Toronto Police Museum ✱

Where? 40 College Street
324-6201
TTC: From College Station walk one block west to Bay Street
When? Open year-round 9 am–9 pm daily
How much? Free
How long? 1 hour
Extras: A store on the main floor sells all kinds of Metropolitan Toronto Police paraphernalia — flashlights, badges, key chains, pens, etc. — that make an unusual gift for a junior Kojak

The Metropolitan Toronto Police Museum is a small, well-designed attraction with plenty to amuse kids and their parents.

The historical section of the museum contains displays of police uniforms, badges, guns, vehicles (including a 1920s paddy wagon), flashlights, nightsticks, you name it. Youngsters can even try out an old-fashioned jail cell, part of a replica of a 1929 police station.

The nuts and bolts of crime solving are laid out in displays of forensic equipment, both current and outmoded. All of this appeals to most kids' natural ghoulishness: they just love the bloodstains and bone fragments. There are cases containing items connected with some of the city's most notorious crimes that will fascinate adults who remember these grisly episodes; some parents, however, may consider them too raw for young children.

Touch-screen video terminals illustrate the complexities of fingerprint identification and the unreliability of eyewitness reports. For the last, you watch

a brief video of a crime being committed, then try to match up your recollections with various suspects; kids seem to score better than adults at this game. Video-screen quizzes on law-enforcement topics like drugs, and films on safety and crime, round out your visit to one of the city's most entertaining and budget-friendly family sites.

Montgomery's Inn

Where? 4709 Dundas Street West, at Islington Avenue 394-8113
TTC: From Islington Station take the Islington bus north
When? Tuesdays–Fridays 9:30 am–4:30 pm, Saturdays and Sundays 1–5 pm, closed Mondays
How much? $2.50 for adults, $1 for children, $6 for families
How long? 1 hour
Extras: Afternoon tea served daily 2–4:30 pm, free parking

Although mid-19th-century guests here complained of high prices, terrible food, and unfriendly servants, today's visitors enjoy better hospitality from the gracious costumed interpreters who staff this Georgian-style stone inn. For kids the most intriguing part of the visit is likely to be the "overnight bedroom" that once housed short-term guests who rented a space in a bed which they often had to share with a

Where's the fire?

Most young children regard firefighting as a great career option and the Toronto Fire Department is happy to nurture this interest by welcoming visits to its firehalls. The public is free to drop in anytime; unless the firefighters are in the middle of responding to an alarm, they will show kids around and let them peek inside those thrilling red fire engines.

The **Toronto Fire Academy** at 895 Eastern Avenue trains firefighters. The building houses a small museum of firefighting that is open from 8 am to 4 pm daily (the museum is scheduled for an upgrade when funds are available). During June, the academy hosts Fire Safety Day at Nathan Phillips Square, and the kids can get an up-close look at equipment and ask questions. The really big show occurs in mid-July, when open house activities at the Fire Academy include watching firefighters extinguish a real blaze of an on-site house used for training purposes. Call 392-1599 for more information.

stranger! The bar room contains some of the simple entertainments that diverted patrons before pinball and video games.

Ontario Legislature (Queen's Park)

Where? 1 Queen's Park 325-7500
TTC: Walk north from Queen's Park Station
When? During the summer, daily tours run roughly hourly between 9 am and 4 pm; the rest of the year tours run weekdays only, on a schedule dictated by demand; often these tours are prebooked by groups, but individuals and families are welcome to tag along
How much? Free
How long? 1–1½ hours
Extras: Cafeteria in basement, souvenir shop, wheelchair and stroller accessible, (except public galleries), limited free parking

Glowering like a Victorian dowager at the top of University Avenue, the Legislative Assembly Building, seat of the provincial government of Ontario, was built in the late 1880s and opened on April 4, 1893. Tours of the building (available in English and French) focus on the main floors of the East and West

Wings and are likely to interest children over ten. Historical portraits and the original wooden mace of the first Ontario Legislature are on view, along with some eclectic and rather musty artifacts. One highlight with kid-appeal is the clear outline of a fossilized dinosaur leg that is visible in a marble column of the West Wing.

The real focus of a trip to Queen's Park is the opportunity to watch the government in action. Legislative sessions are held from March to June and September to December; the public may view the proceedings from the gallery, which is reached by elevator to the fourth floor. Passes for the public gallery must be obtained from the information desk at the entrance to the building.

An intriguing feature of the **Legislative Chamber** is the presence of a gaggle of young pages — grade seven and eight students — who carry messages for the Members and perform other duties. These kids are receiving an up-close lesson in civics and democracy, but the antics of the members during the free-for-all of question period — desk-banging, jeering, and heckling — must be somewhat bewildering at first. These goings-on are perhaps a carry-over from the earlier residents on this site, the inmates of an insane asylum, a handful of whose spirits reputedly still stroll the grounds.

At the reception desk, pick up a pamphlet that details the statues and special markers on the grounds surrounding the building.

Spadina House ✈

Where? 285 Castle Road, east of Casa Loma
392-6910
TTC: Take the St. Clair streetcar to Spadina Road, walk south
When? Mondays–Fridays 9:30 am–4 pm, weekends 12–5 pm; all visitors must take a 45-minute tour, no unsupervised visits permitted
How much? $5 for adults, $3.25 for youths 13–18, $3 for children 6–12, children under 6 free, discounts available if you have visited Casa Loma on the same day
How long? 1 ½ hours
Extras: Fascinating archaeology display in basement, film presentation, gift shop

If you can visit only one of Toronto's historic homes of the once rich and famous, Spadina House, which is the largest, offers the most for your money. This stunning 50-room mansion sits proudly atop a hill overlooking the city, right next door to Casa Loma, and is surrounded in the summer by superb gardens.

Built in 1866, Spadina was the home of the James Austin family, whose descendants lived there until quite recently. Unlike many of the city's other historic houses, Spadina has furnishings, fixtures, and art works that are nearly all original to the home, which was renovated at the turn of the century.

The gardens are remarkable for their variety and the presence of plants that were popular in Victorian horticulture. Maintained by the Toronto Garden Club, the gardens may be toured on Sundays and Wednesdays at 1, 2, and 3 pm. Kids might enjoy taking the long staircase through the trees down to Davenport Road; the climb back up may be less appealing to parents.

Todmorden Mills Heritage Museum and Art Centre

Where? 67 Pottery Road
396-2819

TTC: From Broadview Station take the Cosburn bus north to Pottery Road and walk down the hill

When? Tuesdays–Fridays 10 am–4:30 pm, Saturdays and Sundays 11 am–4:30 pm

How much? $2.25 for adults, $1.75 for students, $1.25 for children 6–12; children under 6 free; visitors may enjoy the grounds and look at the buildings' exteriors for no charge

How long? 1–2 hours with nature walk

Extras: Not recommended for visitors with strollers or wheelchairs; free parking

Although this pastoral site is nestled in the shadow of a busy expressway, it retains the atmosphere of a small late-18th-century settlement. All of the buildings here, except the old Don railway station, are original to the location, which was named by its first inhabitants after their village in Yorkshire, England. The buildings sit adjacent to a nature trail and a unique wildflower preserve, and it's only a short hop along Pottery Road to the Don River bike path, which offers an hour-long stroll right down to the waterfront. Or you can head north along the path to the small waterfall.

This area was originally settled in 1794 and the first buildings were grist mills and sawmills. The large, windowless white building to the right as you enter the site is the **Eastwood-Skinner paper mill**, a building that has been continuously occupied for longer than any other in Toronto; today it is home to a nursery school, among other uses. The two houses at Todmorden are the rustic **Terry Cottage**, built in 1797, and the more imposing **Helliwell House**, which was added to the site in the mid-1800s; both are furnished and open to the public during museum hours.

The **Helliwell Brewery** building, where you pay your admission, offers exhibits of local history and a small gift shop. The picturesque **Don railway station** dates from 1881, and young kids love to play on the small section of tracks beside it. If you enter the nature trail through the woods behind the station, you stand a good chance of spotting some wildlife, as the Don Valley is home to a wide range of animals, including foxes, raccoons, and skunks. In spring, be sure to visit the wild-flower preserve, which is carpeted with white trilliums, the official provincial flower.

Todmorden hosts a variety of special events for families on weekends. During the summer, there are craft workshops for kids aged 6 to 12 on Sunday afternoons; preregistration is required, so call ahead to book your child a spot.

Toronto's First Post Office

Where? 260 Adelaide Street East
865-1833
TTC: Take the King streetcar to Jarvis Street, then walk north to Adelaide Street
When? Mondays–Fridays 9 am–4 pm, Saturdays and Sundays 10 am–4 pm
How much? Free
How long? ½ hour

Opened in 1834, this elegant building houses the oldest working post office in Canada. The interior is fully restored and staffed by costumed interpreters. For a dollar, children can write letters with real quill pens, blot them with

sand, seal them with wax, then mail them on the spot. There are special stamp issues for sale, which are displayed amid exhibits of Canadian postal history. A great place to shop for any junior philatelist.

Sports museums

Hockey Hall of Fame ✱

Where? 30 Yonge Street; enter by the concourse under BCE Place
360-7765
TTC: From Union Station walk one block east to Yonge Street, or from King Station walk south to Front Street
When? Spring and summer: Mondays–Wednesdays 9 am–6 pm, Thursdays and Fridays 9 am–9:30 pm, Saturdays 9 am–6 pm, Sundays 10 am–6 pm; fall and winter: Mondays–Saturdays 9 am–6 pm, Sundays 10 am-6 pm
How much? $8.50 for adults, $5.50 for children 3–13, seniors $5.50
How long? 2 hours
Extras: Excellent souvenir shop for young hockey fans,

111

with every imaginable NHL doodad and a great selection of clothing; wheelchair and stroller accessible; receivers for the hearing impaired; 2 snackbars

The Hockey Hall of Fame, which opened in 1993, has quickly become North America's most visited sports museum. This glitzy, high-impact attraction is located in a restored Bank of Montreal head-office building, originally constructed in the mid-1880s and now integrated in its entirety into the new BCE Place skyscraper complex. The bank's central rotunda was converted into the **Bell Great Hall**, which enshrines the Holy Grail of hockey, the **Stanley Cup**, and a display of the 300 honoured members of the Hall of Fame. The 14 metre-high (45-foot) stained-glass dome is the largest of its kind in Canada.

Below ground on the BCE Concourse level are the exhibits, arranged in 12 zones. There's the Great Moments Zone; the History Zone with its display of 100 years of hockey equipment; the Marquee Zone, which honours hockey's great arenas; the Dressing Room Zone with its full-scale reproduction of the Montreal Canadiens' dressing room, complete to the last jockstrap; the Arena Zone with its tributes to hockey's greatest legends; the Family Zone, which emphasizes the role hockey plays in so many families; the North American Zone, which reveals the extent of non-professional hockey; and the International Zone with artifacts from 32 countries outside of North America (would you believe Australians and South Africans play hockey?).

Unless they are the keenest of fanatics who thrill to the sight of Gordie Howe's uniform or Ken Dryden's mask, most kids will find the zones with interactive displays of greatest appeal. In the Rink Zone, would-be Gretzkys can take to the plastic-ice surface and test the accuracy of their shots, or measure their goaltending prowess while trying to fend off computer-generated shots. The Broadcast Zone gives kids a chance to play Howie Meeker in four fully equipped broadcasting pods and hear their own play-by-play. The museum is also chock-full of computer touch-screens and other interactive media.

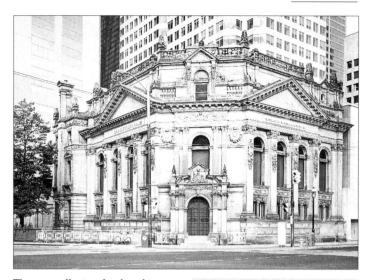

The overall stimulus level is high: don't be surprised if the kids emerge wired. If the weather's good, consider chilling out at the nearby **Berczy Park** near the intersection of Front and Church Streets. There you can admire the trompe l'oeil mural on the back of the **Gooderham Building**, Toronto's own Flatiron.

Canada's Sports Hall of Fame

Where? Exhibition Place (Canadian National Exhibition grounds) 260-6789
TTC: Take the Bathurst streetcar to Exhibition Place
When? Open daily (except major holidays) 10 am–4:30 pm

How much? Free
Extras: Free parking except during the CNE and special events

Canada's greatest athletes, their most memorable moments, and the trophies and tools of their trade come alive on three floors of displays dedicated to outstanding Canadian achievement in amateur and professional sport. Over 50 sports are recognized in the hall's annual induction of members and you can view their sporting triumphs on interactive computer screens. Especially moving is the tribute to Terry Fox, the heroic one-legged runner who undertook a run across Canada to raise funds for cancer research.

113

6: Arts smarts

Many parents who were culture vultures in the years B.C. (before children) reluctantly put aside their interests once they have kids.

But there's no reason to miss out on the riches offered by painting, sculpture, music, dance, and theatre. Kids are just as capable as adults of responding to the arts, and they are often more welcome in art galleries or at performances than you might guess. Toronto's spectrum of cultural activities is vast and diverse; here is a selection of sites that offer memorable experiences for kids and adults alike.

Art galleries

Art Gallery of Ontario ✱

Where? 317 Dundas Street West
979-6648
TTC: From St. Patrick Station walk two blocks west on Dundas Street or take the Dundas streetcar
When? Victoria Day to Thanksgiving: closed Mondays and Tuesdays except holidays; open all other days 10 am–5:30 pm, except Wednesdays 10 am–10 pm. Thanksgiving

to Victoria Day: closed
Mondays (except holidays)
and Tuesdays; open
Wednesdays and Fridays
10 am–10 pm; Thursdays,
Saturdays, Sundays
10 am–5:30 pm
How much? $7.50 for adults,
$4 for students, $15 for a
family of 2 adults and 2
children 12–18; free
admission for children
under 12 accompanied by
an adult; Wednesday
evenings 5–10 pm free to all

How long? 2–4 hours, including a break for a snack
Extras: Gift and bookshop
with excellent range of art
books for children, many
art-related toys, T-shirts,
supplies, and knick-knacks;
gallery is wheelchair and
stroller accessible, strollers
available, licensed restau-
rant/ bar off Sculpture
Court, licensed reasonably
priced cafeteria in base-
ment, baby-changing room
near cafeteria

The city's premier spot for lovers of the visual arts, the Art Gallery of Ontario is a popular family destination that offers inspiring sights for visitors of all ages. From their earliest months, my husband and I have taken our kids to the AGO, initially as an escape from the confinements of being house-bound with infants, then as a pleasant place for toddlers on bad-weather days. To our delight, the boys soon enjoyed the gallery for its intended purpose: they looked forward to viewing the paintings and sculpture and giving their opinions.

Reopened in 1993 after extensive renovations, the Art Gallery of Ontario is a stunning building in its own right, and children respond to its interesting spaces, from the soaring vault of the Tannenbaum Atrium to the small, intimate rooms densely hung with 19th-century paintings.

The wealth and variety of the AGO's collections demand that you be selective if you are to encourage junior art lovers. The following must-sees are recommended for their artistic merit or for their appeal to young sensibilities.

Don't miss the **European Art Galleries** surrounding the beautiful Walker Court (main floor); these house popular works of the 19th-century Impressionists that older kids may recognize.

The **Tannenbaum Atrium** (south side of the main floor) is an airy, glassed-in arcade with massive Rodin sculptures and modern works. If the walls of paintings in the windowless galleries become overwhelming, head here for a breather, or lunch in the Atrium Bar or Gallery Restaurant.

The **Canadian Galleries** (on the upper level) draw in youngsters with their audio-phones and touch-screens. The familiar Group of Seven paintings are presented with lots of engaging gizmos that entertain while educating.

The **Contemporary Art Galleries** bewilder many adults with their modern abstract works, but young children especially react to these spontaneously, without worrying "Is it art?" Don't miss Claes Oldenburg's "Giant Hamburger" (1962) or Roy Liechtenstein's comic-book panels.

The **Henry Moore Sculpture**

Centre (east end of the upper level) is an eye-filling knockout that exercises its magic even on toddlers. Seventeen massive plaster casts by the renowned British sculptor repose in a large unadorned room that is awash in natural light: the sculptures resemble huge fossils in a dinosaur bone-yard and kids love to study them from all angles — just as Moore intended.

Another big draw at the AGO is the **Dr. Mariano Elia Hands On Centre** — also called **Off the Wall!** (on the lower level). This art-play area, open to all kids, provides a creative array of activities that appeal to children from toddler-hood up. There are large magnetic wall-puzzles of famous paintings, build-your-own sculpture areas, a project-

your-own artwork corner, com-puters loaded with the latest in artwork programming, and a dress-up area where kids can be photographed against backdrops from well-known paintings. All of this fun is included with admission to the gallery. Off the Wall! is open Wednesdays 5:30–9:30 pm; Saturdays 1–5 pm; Sundays and holiday Mondays 11 am–5 pm. Parents must remain in the Hands On area to supervise younger children.

At the AGO, every Sunday is Family Sunday, with a host of activities geared to parents and children, all offered at no additional charge. The Sunday Studio program from 1 to 4 pm gives everyone, regardless of age, access to the spectacular Anne Tannenbaum Studio and all its wonderful art-making materials. Visitors get help from artists and volunteers while they experiment with drawing, painting, print-making, and sculpture. There is also a regular Sunday concert by various musicians playing everything from classical concerti to down-and-dirty blues. Child-oriented tours of the different galleries, storytelling, and games complete one of the best shows in town for rainy-day Sundays.

Included with gallery admission is entrance to **The Grange**, Toronto's oldest remaining brick house, built around 1817. Originally the home of the D'Arcy Boulton family, this Georgian-style mansion housed the first Art Gallery of Ontario. It is staffed with interpreters who make children feel welcome with cookies from the kitchen and a scavenger-hunt sheet, which invites them to search for artifacts and utensils.

Parents of younger children, who may tire of the AGO fairly quickly, might find it helpful to promise a visit to **Grange Park**, south of the Grange mansion, as a reward for good beha-viour. The park has an excellent playground and a wading pool, with lots of shady benches for foot-weary art lovers to rest.

If you are looking for a meal or snack in the area, try **Village by the Grange**, a shopping arcade on McCaul Street, east of the AGO, which has an extensive food court featuring a range of tastes: Vietnamese, Afghani, Indonesian, Mexican, Thai, and Greek cuisines are available here and at very reasonable prices. There are also good restaurants north of the gallery, on Baldwin Street. Also not far from the gallery are the Queen Street West Village (see page 193), Chinatown (see page 197), and Kensington Market (see page 198).

McMichael Canadian Art Collection ✱

Where? Islington Avenue, Kleinburg
905-893-1121
Transit: Penetang-Midland Coach Lines operates a bus from the Coach Terminal at Bay and Dundas Streets and from the Yorkdale GO Station, six days a week,

leaving Bay Street at 10:45 am and Yorkdale at 11:15 am; for more information call the gallery

When? June 1–October 31: 10 am–5 pm daily; November 1–May 31: Tuesdays–Sundays 10 am–4 pm; gallery tours Saturdays, Sundays, and holiday Mondays at 1 and 3 pm

How much? $6 for adults, $3 for children 5–18, kids under 5 free, $13 for families (up to 2 adults and kids under 18)

How long? 2–4 hours, with a break for a snack and a walk

Extras: Restaurant, cafeteria, free parking, excellent gift shop, beautiful grounds for family hiking and picnicking

If you are looking for an excursion outside the city that combines art, scenery, hiking, and small-town browsing, head for the McMichael Canadian Art Collection in Kleinburg, about 60 minutes north of downtown Toronto.

The McMichael Collection grew out of a private collection of works by the Group of Seven, and today the gallery is a national showcase for exclusively Canadian art, including an impressive range of works by native artists. The collection is housed in an attractive stone and wood building, that has little of the usual formality of a major museum; visitors relax immediately in its cottage-like warmth and attractive open spaces.

Curators and programmers have gone out of their way to make the McMichael kid-friendly, offering Family Packs of activities and objects that enhance children's experience of the gallery. There is a hands-on display of native art on the second floor that invites kids to touch the works and to answer a quiz. Also on the second floor is a weekend drop-in art centre where young visitors can experiment with various media and participate in a scheduled craft under the supervision of McMichael staff. The second Sunday of every month is Family Day, with activities, workshops, films, and performances; some of these take place outside on the beautiful grounds during the warm months. The gallery holds special activities during Christmas and March Break, and on such holidays as Canada Day and Mother's Day.

A trip to the McMichael is more than just an opportunity to look at paintings. There is a comfortable restaurant with a gorgeous view over rolling hills (not to be missed in the fall) and reasonably priced, wholesome food. A large shop sells all kinds of Canadiana gifts and a solid selection of children's books. The shack where Group of Seven member Tom Thomson used to paint is located on the grounds, moved here from its original spot in Toronto's Rosedale Valley.

No visit would be complete without a stroll to the Humber River Valley, behind the gallery. If you follow the path down the hill and along the river, you'll end up at a municipal playground in Kleinburg, a town that also has several antique stores, specialty shops, and pleasant restaurants for visitors looking to make a day of their visit to the McMichael Collection.

The Market Gallery

Where? 95 Front Street East 392-7604
TTC: From Union Station walk two blocks east to Jarvis Street
When? Wednesdays–Fridays 10 am–4 pm, Saturdays 9 am–4 pm, Sundays 12–4 pm
How much? Free
How long? ½ hour

This second-floor gallery space in the south building of the St. Lawrence Market is a great place to combine the viewing of paintings and photography with the purchase of the weekly rations from the butchers, bakers, and greengrocers below. The Market Gallery belongs to the City of Toronto and its exhibitions are drawn from works in the city's archives and art collections. These provide fascinating insights into local history, and visitors with children will feel comfortable in the casual atmosphere of the gallery.

Private galleries

Toronto has scores of privately owned galleries that are open to the public. Most are concentrated in the Bloor-Yorkville area, in the Queen Street West Village, and along King Street West near Dufferin Street, with smatterings in other neighbourhoods. It costs nothing to visit these galleries, and many local art lovers make a day of gallery-hopping during the fall and spring openings seasons. I have always found that gallery owners welcome well-supervised children and are eager to share their love of art with a new generation of potential connoisseurs.

Of the numerous private galleries in the city, the ones listed below deserve special mention.

Check the Yellow Pages for the addresses of other private galleries; note that most are closed on Sundays and Mondays.

Animation Gallery
Queen's Quay Terminal, Harbourfront
203-3858

World of Animation
1977 Queen Street East
691-4105
Most kids love cartoons and they'll also love these unique galleries devoted to original animation art. All the usual suspects from Disney, Warner Brothers, and Hanna-Barbera can be found here, along with lesser-known characters. Visitors can see the painstaking process by which cartoons were created in precomputer times.

Isaacs/Innuit Gallery
9 Prince Arthur Avenue
921-9985
Innuit art with its emphasis on animals and human figures is

121

Children's books

Toronto is remarkable for the number of specialty children's bookstores it supports. The local presence of several internationally recognized children's publishers, such as Kids Can Press and Annick Press; of the Canadian Children's Book Centre, which promotes our national children's literature; and of a lively community of authors and illustrators contributes to this enthusiasm for kids' books. Whatever the reason, the results are wonderful for parents trying to foster a love of reading.

The Canadian Children's Book Centre
35 Spadina Road
975-0010
This non-profit organization sponsors numerous activities that celebrate and promote the excellence of Canadian authored and illustrated books. First among these is the Canadian Children's Book Week, an annual national festival featuring author and illustrator visits to libraries, bookstores, and community centres across Canada. For parents, two of the centre's many publications, which can be ordered, are especially useful: *Our Choice*, an annual roundup of the best Canadian kids' titles published that year, along with a selected backlist from the previous two years, and *Too Good to Miss*, an annotated 200-title list of classic Canadian children's books.

immensely appealing to kids. Hailed as the finest gallery of Innuit art in the world, the Isaacs/Innuit has a rich variety of sculpture, prints, drawings, and wall hangings for everyone to enjoy. It's just around the corner from the Royal Ontario Museum and well worth a small detour.

Jane Corkin Gallery
179 John Street
979-1980
Toronto's most prominent gallery of historical and contemporary photography often has exhibitions that

122

Active Minds

This bookstore chain operates stores in three suburban shopping malls: Sherway, Erin Mills, and Fairview. In addition to books, the stores sell a wide range of toys, games, and activity sets, and are a great place for one-stop gift shopping.

The Children's Book Store

2532 Yonge Street
480-0233

Dubbed "the Louvre of kiddie-lit," this is a three-star, don't-miss attraction for families who treasure books. Free entertainment most weekends. (See page 131.)

Parentbooks

201 Harbord Street 537-8334

Nobody ever said raising children was easy, but whatever your problem of the moment — from pregnancy to adolescence — the excellently stocked Parentbooks has a title to help you through it. Other bookstores to visit:

Mabel's Fables
662 Mount Pleasant Road
322-0438
2939 Bloor Street West
233-8830
Tiddely Pom Books
for Children
47A Colborne Street
366-0290
The Lion, The Witch
and The Wardrobe
888 Eglinton Avenue West
785-9177

intrigue youngsters, teaching them that there's more to photography than the family snapshot. Located near the Art Gallery of Ontario, just north of the Queen Street West Village, the Corkin Gallery makes a pleasant addition to the art-loving family's itinerary.

80 Spadina

80 Spadina Avenue,
south of King Street

This rehabilitated old office building houses several galleries and makes a great browser's destination. You can see a lot of art — paintings,

123

sculpture, and photography — ranging from the traditional to the most avant-garde all under one roof. There's even a pleasant café where art lovers congregate to discuss the current shows.

Theatre

Toronto ranks as the world's third-largest English-language theatre centre after London and New York. The city has over 40 professional theatres encompassing everything from the Victorian elegance of the Royal Alexandra to the sleek modernity of the Ford Centre for the Performing Arts in North York. You can watch plays in converted warehouses, renovated churches, or under the stars. A production of Shakespeare's *Romeo and Juliet* was recently mounted under a highway overpass, with street people as actors.

In recent years, Toronto has become home to several long-running mega-hits like *Phantom of the Opera*, *Miss Saigon*, and *Show Boat*. Although some critics bemoan this trend for diverting audiences from more original, local companies, there's no denying that the lavish theatricality of these productions can arouse the interest of young audiences in the magic of live theatre.

Theatre tickets, especially for the larger productions, can be expensive. One way to lower the cost of taking the whole family to a show is to check out the **Five Star Tickets booth** (596-8211), located outside the Eaton Centre at Yonge and Dundas Streets, for same-

day, reduced-price tickets. The booth posts a list of the shows for which it has such tickets and the offerings change daily. Tickets are sold on a cash-only, no-return-or-exchange basis for that day's performance.

Young People's Theatre ✱

Where? 165 Front Street East
Reception: 363-5131
Box office: 862-2222
TTC: From Union Station walk east along Front Street
When? Evening and daytime performances, from October through May; no shows during the summer
How much? Call the box office for ticket prices; tickets range from $15 to $30, depending on the show; Pay What You Can performances are scheduled for some productions, with PWYC tickets sold one hour before the performance begins

The primary venue for children's theatre in Toronto is the Young People's Theatre, the largest theatre in Canada focusing exclusively on producing plays for young people and their families. The theatre on Front Street was built in 1977 within the shell of a building that was originally constructed in 1881 as a stable for the Toronto Street Railway's 500 horses, the animals that pulled the company's streetcars. The award-winning renovations preserved the historic exterior while converting the interior to a 300-seat theatre and studio space. The theatre has since been enlarged to 486 seats, and the building also houses a theatre school for children.

Programming at the YPT is varied and thoughtful. New Canadian plays mix with classics like the seasonal production of *A Christmas Carol* and an action-packed *Macbeth* that might make a Shakespeare fan out of your young teenager. Each production is targeted for specific age groups; when you call, ask whether the current play is suited to your children's age range. If you visit the city during Arts Week in late September, check out YPT's fall fair, a free street extravaganza that features live music, face painting, play performances, dancing, and a sale of YPT costumes — just the thing for Halloween.

Shakespeare in the Park

Every summer the Canadian Stage Company mounts a full open-air production of a Shakespeare play in High Park in the city's west end (see page 137). The atmosphere is informal; kids may prefer this introduction to the great playwright to sitting still in a theatre. And you can always head for the playground if younger members of the audience get too restless. Call 368-3110.

Theatre tours

Although you may not feel you can afford to take the whole family to an extravaganza like *Phantom of the Opera*, a few of the larger theatres offer tours that give visitors a behind-the-scenes look at how a large production is mounted. Any kid who has ever fantasized about performing or who has been enchanted by the illusion of live theatre should find these tours rewarding. Recommended for children over seven years.

Elgin and Winter Garden Theatres

Where? 189 Yonge Street
365-5353
TTC: From Queen Station walk north on Yonge Street
When? Tours Thursdays at 5 pm, Saturdays at 11 am; additional tours during July and August, Sundays at 11 am
How much? $4 for adults, $2.50 for children
How long? Tour lasts 1½ hours

Together these two theatres represent a unique restoration site: the only "double-decker" theatre complex ever built in Canada. The downstairs Elgin Theatre opened in 1913 as Loew's Yonge Street Theatre and was the city's premier vaudeville house. Sumptuous in its decor, with lavishly gilded plasterwork and damask wall coverings, the 1500-seat Elgin is a knockout. Upstairs, the Winter Garden Theatre is a fantastical space right out of a fairy tale: an enchanted forest with 5000 painted beech leaves hanging from the ceiling and bedecked with multi-coloured lanterns.

The tour gives fascinating details about the restoration, such as how hundreds of volunteers were recruited to roll bread dough over the Winter Garden's walls to remove 60 years of grime. Guides deliver a brief history of vaudeville, show historical photos and artifacts like costumes, and explain the workings of the original lighting and projection equipment. The theatre complex also houses the world's largest collection of vaudeville scenery.

Pantages Theatre

Where? 263 Yonge Street
362-3218
TTC: From Dundas Station walk south on Yonge Street
When? Tours at 11:30 am daily except Wednesdays and Saturdays, when a video presentation is at 10:30 am
How much? $4 per person
How long? 1 hour

Constructed in 1919, the Pantages was once the largest vaudeville theatre in the British Empire. Like the Elgin, it dates from an era that tended towards the grandiose in theatre design. The one-hour tour reveals some of the technical wizardry behind the current high-glitz production, *Phantom of the Opera*, which is the first and only show the recently renovated (1990) theatre has mounted.

Roy Thomson Hall

Where? 60 Simcoe Street
Box office: 872-4255
Tours: 593-4822
TTC: From St. Andrew
Station walk west one block
on King Street
When? Daily tours at 12:30
pm, except Wednesdays
and Sundays
How much? $3 per person
Extras: For the junior
virtuoso, visit the MusicStore
in the hall lobby; the selection of children's music on
tape and CD is excellent and
there are also lots of music-
related gifts and knick-knacks

This is the city's prime venue

for classical music and home to
the internationally acclaimed
Toronto Symphony Orchestra.
Roy Thomson Hall is situated
in a lively theatre district close
to the Royal Alexandra and
Princess of Wales theatres, the
new Canadian Broadcasting
Corporation headquarters, and
Metro Hall. Designed by Arthur
Erickson, the concert hall's
exterior is an airy construction
of glass and steel. In contrast to
the lavish reds and golds of the
Edwardian theatres, RTH's
interior is a calming soft grey
throughout. The lobby houses
the grand piano of Canadian
musical legend Glenn Gould.

The main focus of the 45-
minute tour is an explanation

of the hall's acoustic features, which include 30 acrylic discs that hang over the stage to be raised or lowered as needed. Hundreds of tubular banners suspended from the ceiling act as sound absorbers and look to kids like hanging cigars.

If you want to hear some music at Roy Thomson Hall but are wary of ticket prices that run between $25 and $75 for evening symphony concerts, check out the Evening Over-tures chamber music concerts that are occasionally performed by small groups of symphony artists before the main concerts. These 45-minute concerts offer excellent value for only $4.50 a ticket. Or try to catch a free BYOL (Bring Your Own Lunch) concert, by young musicians, on Fridays at noon in the lobby, from October to April.

Classical music and dance

Toronto Symphony Orchestra Young People's Concerts
Roy Thomson Hall
60 Simcoe Street
598-3375

During the Toronto Symphony Orchestra's regular season at Roy Thomson Hall, which runs from mid-September through May, there are a number of Saturday-afternoon concerts specifically designated for audiences aged seven to twelve. These are full symphony performances that give children an introduction to the excitement of a large-orchestra sound in a concert-hall setting. The programs blend classical music with a mix of drama, clowning, storytelling, mime, or puppetry. The concerts are often preceded by "mini-concerts" performed by young musicians in the Roy Thomson Hall lobby. Series tickets for five concerts cost around $50; individual tickets are also available.

Cushion Concerts
Harbourfront
973-4000
From November through May, Harbourfront hosts a twice-monthly series of concerts that offer classical music, dance, and storytelling from the Western tradition and other cultures. The Saturday-morning (11 am) concerts are intended for kids between five and eight years old; Sunday-

afternoon (2 pm) concerts are for kids aged eight and over; all tickets are priced at $7.

National Ballet School

105 Maitland Street
962-0945

The country's pre-eminent training ground for classical dancers schedules regular free tours of its school, a wonderful opportunity for young balletomanes to see what goes into the making of a prima ballerina or premier danseur. Visitors can watch ballet classes in progress in this top-notch facility, from September through July, on Wednesdays at 3 pm and Fridays at 10:30 am. Call ahead to make sure that classes are in session, as tours are cancelled during school breaks. The school also mounts public performances by dancers in training at its Betty Oliphant Theatre, during the third week in May.

Performances by children

The city has three internationally acclaimed performance groups that are composed entirely of children. They always win rave reviews from critics and young audiences alike, who are inspired by the high level of professionalism shown by these talented youngsters. Performances occur at different times throughout the year, and Christmas programs are annual treats.

Toronto Children's Chorus

Concerts by this 275-voice professional children's choir are a joy for anyone who loves choral music. The choir performs a varied and sophisticated repertoire of classical and contemporary works, and sometimes accompanies the city's renowned Toronto Mendelssohn Choir. Call 932-8666.

Canadian Children's Opera Chorus

Whenever the Canadian Opera Company needs children's voices, it calls on the CCOC. The chorus's main choir has 75 voices, with children ranging in age from ten to sixteen. The CCOC, which provides both voice and dramatic training, also performs at other events including productions at Harbourfront. Call 366-0467.

Canadian Children's Dance Theatre

This troupe of 16 dancers aged eight to eighteen has been called a "national treasure" by critics for its exuberant style and choreography. The CCDT performs its Christmas classic *WindSong* at the Premiere Dance Theatre during December and other repertoire at Harbourfront's Milk International Festival in May, with additional occasional performances during the year. Call 924-5657.

Literature

The Osborne Collection of Early Children's Books

239 College Street
393-7753

The Osborne is a unique national collection of children's books ranging from a 14th-century volume of Aesop's Fables to materials pertaining to contemporary Canadian children's authors. From a youngster's point of view there is little to see, as the materials are for research purposes only and kept under lock and key, but the librarians do mount small exhibitions of things like Victorian games or old pop-up books that might interest a young bibliophile.

The Children's Book Store ✱

2532 Yonge Street
480-0233

This midtown bookstore, housed in a historic art deco building, is an internationally recognized mecca for young readers. With 25,000 titles in stock and a huge array of children's audio-visual materials, there's very little you won't find here, and if it's not in stock the staff will be happy to order it for you. The largest store of its kind in the world, the Children's Book Store is more than a place to sell books. On the weekends from fall through spring, the store hosts live entertainment by some of Canada's favourite children's performers and appearances by our best-loved authors and illustrators. These events are generally free and take place in mid-afternoon. Call the store to have an events brochure mailed to your home.

7: The great outdoors

hile the pace of urban
growth in Toronto has been dizzying in recent decades,
the city still boasts an exceptional number and variety of
parks and natural areas. Toronto's topography is one of
its greatest assets: the numerous ravines that slice
through the city remain undeveloped and most are home
to many species of plant and animal life.

There are lots of activities in the city's parks throughout the year. For information call City of Toronto Department of Parks and Recreation (392-1111) or Metropolitan Toronto Department of Parks and Property (392-8186). Both publish excellent maps of the parks under their jurisdiction, which are available by mail. City of Toronto Department of Parks sponsors a Summer Music Festival at various of its locations; a brochure listing these free daytime and evening concerts is yours for the asking.

Whether you want to stroll on a lakeside boardwalk, scale a bluff, hike through pristine woods, listen to jazz al fresco, launch a boat, play baseball, sniff roses, or pet baby pigs, Toronto parks have something for everyone — and most of the time it's free. The parks listed below are located mainly in the downtown or midtown area and are easily reached by public transit.

Allan Gardens

Where? Carlton Street between Jarvis and Sherbourne Streets
392-1111

TTC: From College Station take the College/Carlton streetcar east to Sherbourne Street, or from Sherbourne Station take the Sherbourne bus south to Carlton Street

When? 10 am–5 pm daily

How much? Free

How long? 1 hour

Extras: Free parking at rear, washrooms, greenhouse is wheelchair and stroller accessible

The large domed greenhouse in the centre of this downtown park is reminiscent of Joseph Paxton's 19th-century Crystal Palace in London and summons memories of Victorian Toronto, when this now rather neglected area was home to prominent families like the Masseys and the Jarvises. The greenhouse is worth a visit at any time of year but really comes into its own in the depths of a Toronto

winter, when its steamy warmth and profusion of colour are most keenly appreciated. Kids love the humongous goldfish in the fishponds and marvel at the exotic fruit-bearing tropical trees, while adults can admire

133

the overall artistry of the gardens' layout.

If younger children have had enough of botany, there is a small outdoor playground at the south end of the building. The large park around the greenhouse, while certainly safe during the daytime, is home to many of the area's transients and you can expect to be hit up for spare change. At night, this area becomes a prostitutes' stroll: an evening outing *en famille* is not recommended.

The Beaches Parks ✱

Where? Along the lakeshore, between Coxwell and Victoria Park Avenues
TTC: Take the Queen streetcar to Kew Gardens and walk south through the park to the boardwalk

A unique chain of parks runs along Lake Ontario from the foot of Coxwell Avenue east to Victoria Park Avenue, connected by a continuous boardwalk beloved by dog-walkers, joggers, hand-in-hand teenagers, and Torontonians of all stripes. You can combine your boardwalk stroll with playground visits, sandcastle building, a

game of tennis or beach volleyball, a fitness workout, a pool swim or wading-pool splash, and a foray up to Queen Street's many shops and restaurants (see page 193).

If you are travelling by car, your best chance of finding a parking spot is in the lot at the foot of Coxwell Avenue, which is also an ideal starting point to explore the Beaches parks. By the lot is the **Boardwalk Restaurant**, a popular local eatery with a slightly upscale burgers-and-pasta-type menu. Its large outdoor patio is a great spot to catch the lake breezes on a humid evening.

West of the parking lot is **Ashbridge's Bay Park**, which curves around a peninsula that ends in a rocky outcropping and small beach that usually afford a quiet spot for the kids to paddle about or toss tidbits to the ravenous gulls. Ashbridge's Bay also has a large marina and a wading pool. Retracing your steps east along the boardwalk, you'll come to **Woodbine Beach**, a wide sweep of sand beach, heavily populated with sunbathers and volleyball players in the summer months. Further east, you'll find the **Donald D.**

Summerville Olympic Pool. On the pool building's boardwalk level there's a place to rent windsurfing gear and sign up for some lessons. A playground adjoins the pool complex, which also houses a fast-food outlet during the warm months.

Keep walking east along the boardwalk until you reach **Kew Gardens Park**, which runs from Queen Street down to the boardwalk and is the centrepiece of the Beaches park chain with its tennis courts, ice rink, playground, wading pool, lawn-bowling greens, bandstand, and Beaches Library. A snackbar located on the boardwalk at the south end of Kew Gardens operates seasonally.

The picturesque gardener's cottage on the park's eastern periphery is a much-treasured local landmark.

The boardwalk continues along the lake, separating park areas from the beach, until it ends at Silver Birch Avenue, ten blocks east of Kew Gardens. Here you'll find another playground, the (private) **Balmy Beach Canoe Club**, and a second snackbar. Head up any of the streets that run north from the lake to admire the neighbourhood's eclectic architecture along the way; then enjoy a bite at one of Queen Street's many inviting cafés. The complete boardwalk route is 3 kilometres (2 miles) one way.

Edwards Gardens and Civic Garden Centre

Where? 777 Lawrence Avenue East
397-1340
TTC: From Lawrence Station take the Lawrence East bus to Leslie Street
When? Civic Garden Centre is open year-round; April 1–Thanksgiving: Mondays–Fridays 9:30 am–5 pm, Saturdays and Sundays 12–5 pm; winter hours: Mondays–Fridays 9:30 am–4 pm, Saturdays and Sundays 12–4 pm. Free tours of the gardens are offered in season twice weekly, Tuesdays and Thursdays; call the Civic Garden Centre for precise times.
How much? Free
How long? 1–3 hours, depending on how far you choose to walk
Extras: Free parking, licensed snackbar, gift shop
Note: Bicycles and dogs are prohibited

Edwards Gardens, Toronto's largest public gardens, are a popular spot for family outings and the taking of wedding photographs. Although the gardens are modest in comparison with the Butchart Gardens in Victoria, British Columbia, or the huge Royal Botanical Gardens in Hamilton, Ontario, there is a duckpond and lots of paths for kids to run off some energy while their parents enjoy the flora. Wheelchair- and stroller-accessible routes are clearly marked.

Edwards Gardens are at the north end of the Central Don parks system, a long chain of ravine parks that allows cyclists and hikers to travel from Lawrence Avenue right down to the waterfront. If you are looking for a longer walk beyond the gardens, locate the access point marked **Wilket Creek Park** at the park's south end, and follow the cycling/walking path along the creek. It's a 5-kilometre (3-mile) walk down to Eglinton Avenue and you might spot some wildlife along the way. My kids were thrilled to discover a large turtle in the creek, next to what looked like a beaver or muskrat lodge.

The **Civic Garden Centre** is action central for Metro's

gardeners, operating as a meeting place for various horticultural societies and offering frequent educational programs and flower shows. The shop on the lower level carries a worthy selection of books of interest to young naturalists and gardeners.

High Park ♣

Where? Bloor Street West, across from High Park Station
Note: No cars permitted in the park on Sundays and holidays

This 160-hectare (400-acre) park is a great destination for a full-day family outing, offering a wealth of activities — all of them free or inexpensive — to suit different ages.

For a fascinating look at history, visit High Park's **Colborne Lodge** (see page 97); this house is open to the public and has been restored, with many original furnishings and artifacts, to the 1870s period.

There are two playgrounds in the park, one in the north-west quadrant near Bloor Street and a second in the southeast near Parkside Drive. The latter has a long hillside slide that kids can't resist; the other has a wading pool. Across Spring Road from the south playground are the duckponds, home to hundreds of waterfowl who owe their rather corpulent appearance to the park visitors' generous bags of breadcrumbs and popcorn.

Heading west along Deer Pen Road, you'll come across the park's animal paddocks, a mini-zoo containing deer,

137

Local heroes

Baseball

The Toronto Blue Jays, the 1992 and 1993 World Series champions, play their regular season at SkyDome from April through September.

Tickets are expensive; a family of four will be hard pressed to pay less than $100 for reasonable seats. For Saturday-afternoon games and a small number of early (starting at 12:35 pm) weekend games, there are Junior Jays half-price tickets for kids under 14. Call 341-1111.

Football

The Toronto Argonauts, recently owned by hockey star Wayne Gretzky and the late, great comic actor John Candy, also play at SkyDome, from late June through October. There are no special discounts for children, but students with a valid ID card can purchase a $10 ticket for a reduced price. Call 341-ARGO.

Hockey

The Toronto Maple Leafs play at the legendary hockey mecca Maple Leaf Gardens, at Carlton and Church Streets. The Leafs are popular, even when they're losing, and tickets are always hard to get. Most seats are reserved for season (October–April) ticket holders; usually the only seats left over are up in the "greys" for around $20. There are no discounted tickets. Call 977-1461.

Basketball

The Toronto Raptors are newcomers to the Toronto professional sports scene. The NBA team will be playing their games at SkyDome in 1995 and 1996, pending the completion of their own facility (location not yet confirmed). Call 214-2255.

bison, llamas, mountain sheep, and goats. They just don't make zoos like this any more — and possibly for good reason — but it's hard not to share the enjoyment that very young kids derive from watching animals even as mundane as these.

At the top of Deer Pen Road you will find the **Grenadier** restaurant, which serves both light take-out snacks and leisurely dinners. But don't expect to relax over a glass of wine; the provisions of Colborne Lodge owner John Howard's will, by which the core of the present parkland was donated to the city, forbids in perpetuity the serving of alcoholic beverages in the park.

From the restaurant and at several other points in the park, you can flag down the trackless train that tours throughout the park. The train takes 20 minutes to complete a loop, but riders are free to hop off and on at a variety of points. Tickets, which can be purchased from the driver, are good for the whole day. The train is the easiest way to reach the shores of **Grenadier Pond**, a natural inlet from Lake Ontario that offers sport fishing to licensed anglers, who can

hope to catch pike, bass, sunfish, and bullheads. This is also a popular spot for model-boat sailing, and in winter the pond doubles as a huge skating rink. From the train you'll see lots of paths through the woods that invite exploring, if you are willing to do some moderate climbing.

Every summer High Park is the venue for a free "Shakespeare Under the Stars" production (see page 126). The plays are presented by professional actors in an open-air amphitheatre just east of the Grenadier restaurant, and they attract enthusiastic audiences of up to 2000 people. Get there early to stake out a spot, and bring a picnic. This is an inexpensive and fun way to introduce children to classical theatre, even if they don't have the staying power to make it to the final curtain. Call 368-3110 for more information.

Besides hiking and cycling, High Park offers numerous sports activities. A sports complex near Bloor Street includes a swimming pool, ice rink, baseball diamond, tennis courts, and fields for football and soccer. Some facilities may be reserved by groups with permits; call 392-1111 to check availability.

James Gardens and Lambton Woods

Where? Edenbridge Drive (off Royal York Road, south of Eglinton Avenue)
TTC: From Royal York Station take the Royal York bus
Note: Bicycles and dogs are prohibited in James Gardens but permitted on the walking/cycling route.

These terraced gardens in a west-end park are Toronto's loveliest, and on weekends they are thronged by camera enthusiasts in search of the perfect photo and amateur artists sketching the graceful arrangements of flower beds. There is a lush variety of flowers, shrubs, and ornamental grasses, with plantings divided by small waterfalls and spring-fed pools arched by picturesque footbridges. The overall effect is gorgeous from early spring through late fall.

If you follow the main path south along the Humber River for a few minutes — perhaps stopping to feed the greedy ducks along the way — you'll see the sign for Lambton Woods, an urban forest of immense diversity that is rich in wildflowers and birds. James Gardens are part of the Tommy Thompson Trail, which links the Humber River parks chain with the lakefront, so it's possible to make a day of walking and picnicking along the trail.

Kortright Centre for Conservation ✱

Where? Pine Valley Drive, Kleinburg
905-832-2289, or 661-6600 for recorded information
Transit: Accessible by car only
When? 10 am–4 pm daily except December 24 and 25; guided walks take place daily at 1 pm, 11:30 am, and 2:30 pm on weekends;
1 pm Mondays to Fridays
How much? $4.25 for adults, $2.50 for children 5–18, children 4 and under free
Extras: Snackbar, picnic area, shop with nature-related gifts, interactive exhibits, theatre showing short films about nature and ecology; building and most trails are wheelchair and stroller accessible; free parking

There is no better place for an outdoor family outing than the Kortright, a 324-hectare (800-acre) site just beyond the northern border of Metro Toronto. Dedicated to nurturing and expanding our understanding of nature and ecology, the centre has year-round exhibits and activities that take advantage of the seasons to promote the message of natural conservation.

The centre offers 18 kilometres (11 miles) of walking trails that lead through forests to marshes, maple-sugar shacks, ponds, and creeks. On weekends, the 1 pm guided hike is designed expressly for kids, who are encouraged to pose questions to the friendly naturalist guides. Themes for these hikes vary throughout the year and might include In Search of Winter Wildlife, Pond Life, Busy Bees (at the centre's apiary), or Fall Colours. From the first weekend in March through to Easter there are maple-syrup demonstrations. March Break is Kortright's busiest week, with ongoing indoor and outdoor activities every day for kids.

One of the more popular hiking routes leads from the centre's main building down through forest to the Humber River floodplain, then continues to a large marsh that you can circle on a boardwalk, keeping an eye out for migrating waterfowl. The trail is well marked and could be done with an extra-sturdy stroller,

but the walk back up would pose a fitness challenge. If you are visiting Kortright with a baby or toddler, a backpack carrier is recommended.

The centre also operates wonderful evening programs about once a month, opportunities to go out in the woods at night to see and hear screech-owls, bats, even foxes and coyotes. If your kids are old enough and aren't afraid of venturing into a dark forest, these programs make for memorable occasions. Advance tickets are required.

Twice a year the Kortright organizes 5-kilometre (3-mile) hikes to the nearby McMichael Canadian Art Collection. Described by the gallery as "moderately strenuous," the hikes appeal to naturalists because they pass through areas of the centre that are not normally open to the public. There is a fee for these hikes; they are suitable only for adults and older children.

Leslie Street Spit

Where? At the foot of Leslie Street, south of Lakeshore Boulevard
661-6600 for access info

TTC: Take the Queen street-car to Leslie Street, then walk south to the park entrance
When? Weekends and holidays year-round 9 am–6 pm, closed on weekdays
Note: No dogs allowed

Officially called **Tommy Thompson Park**, the Leslie Street Spit originated in the 1950s as a landfill dump. Situated on a 5-kilometre (3-mile) peninsula jutting into Lake Ontario, the park is especially suited to cycling and ideal for strollers with its entirely flat terrain. Over the years the dumped rubble was colonized by an unusual variety of plants and these in turn have attracted numerous bird species. Today the spit is a bird sanctuary and an environmentally protected area; some spots are off limits to visitors during nesting season. Over 250 species of birds have been identified here and the ring-billed gull colony is one of the world's largest, numbering around 100,000 nesting pairs. The TTC operates a free shuttle bus from the park's gates to the end of the spit on weekends and holidays in the summer.

Riverdale Farm ✱

Where? 201 Winchester Street
392-6794
TTC: Take the College/
Carlton streetcar to Sumach
Street and walk north along
Sumach to Winchester Street
When? Open daily at 9 am;
variable closing between 4
pm and 6 pm, depending on
the season
How much? Free
Extras: Wading pool in adjacent park; across the street
from the Toronto Necropolis,
a historic cemetery

Perched on the edge of a
ravine that slopes down to the
Don Valley, this 19th-century
working farm offers city kids a
day in the country with its
barns, old-fashioned farm
implements, and picture-pretty
millponds and gardens. The
farm operates as an agricultural education centre, and the
farmers who work there are
happy to answer questions
and introduce young visitors to
the latest arrivals among the
animals, perhaps a litter of
baby piglets or a new calf.
There are all the usual barnyard suspects: horses,
donkeys, sheep, goats, cattle,
and poultry. Many of the
animals can be petted — but
no feeding, please.

The **Simpson House** at the
farm's entrance echoes the
Victorian architecture of the
surrounding Cabbagetown
neighbourhood, with its gingerbread decoration and

143

lovely brickwork. Inside there are washrooms; at the back, a shaded picnic area. At the east end of the farm, look for a large chalet structure that houses an interpretive centre. Here you'll find drop-in craft activities and demonstrations for children every day during the summer and on weekends and holidays during the rest of the year. These excellent work-shops are free and supervised by the farm staff. In fall and spring, Riverdale Farm offers a popular "Young Farmers" program on weekends; it teaches kids all kinds of farm skills and lore. Preregistration is required; call the farm for further details.

It's possible to mix your visit to the farm with a bit of urban hiking. Head down the hill behind the interpretive centre past a forested wildlife sanctu-ary and you'll come upon a picturesque duckpond with an arched stone bridge. On the other side is a gate that leads to a pedestrian walkway over the Don Valley. Take one of the staircases down to the Don River bike path or cross over the bridge to Broadview Avenue. Sometimes this gate is closed; check with farm staff before

leaving the interpretive centre.

If hunger strikes, head south on Broadview Avenue a couple of blocks to Gerrard Street, the heart of one of the city's lively Asian areas. There are lots of places to pick up a quick and cheap Chinese or Vietnamese meal. If you just want to rest quietly for a while, visit the **Riverdale Library** at the corner of Broadview and Gerrard.

The other possibility is to head north on Sumach Street from Riverdale Farm and enjoy the charm of the area's lovely renovated Victorian homes. At the top of Sumach, turn right and you'll reach **Hillsdale Park**, which has a playground, wading pool, and walking trails down to the Don Valley.

Scarborough Bluffs

Where? South of Kingston Road, between Danforth Avenue and Cathedral Bluffs Drive
TTC: From Victoria Park Station, take the Kingston Road bus to Brimley and walk south

Bluffers Park, at the foot of Brimley Road, is the centre-piece of the Scarborough Bluffs parks chain, which runs east — with some interruptions — from south of Danforth and Kingston Roads to Highland Creek. Bluffers Park houses a marina, public washrooms with diaper-changing tables, an outdoor snackbar, a pub/café, and a dining room (food services seasonal). A walking path takes you around the shoreline, but the more daring will want to try scaling the bluffs from the beaches to the east of the park. Older kids should have little trouble making the ascent on their own; younger children, however, should be accompanied.

Cathedral Bluffs Park, at the foot of Cathedral Bluffs Drive, best reached by car, offers the most panoramic views from 30 metres (100 feet) up, but watch the little ones: the drop is precipitous and in places there is no fence. The huge, wide-open field here is ideal to let loose in, as is the great all-ages playground.

Sherwood Park

Where? Sherwood Avenue, near Mount Pleasant and Eglinton Avenues
TTC: From St. Clair Station take the Nortown bus

Tucked behind one of the city's most pleasant midtown neighbourhoods, Sherwood Park is in the middle of a chain of parks that offer great hiking through mature forests and up and down ravines.

A good place to start is the parking lot at the end of Sherwood Avenue, where there's a long walk down a paved drive that leads to a large playground complete with a wading pool and picnic area. At the south end of the playground area, follow the nature trail sign; it will point you in the direction of an easily followed trail through leafy forests alongside a stream. There are lots of offshoot paths to follow for the more adventurous, and on a weekday you will feel far from the city's hubbub. You'll emerge at Bayview Avenue, north of Eglinton Avenue, and can continue north through Sunnybrook Park, but the trail gets steeper and most children will have had enough by now. It goes without saying that the dense deciduous forest makes this walk spectacular in the fall. In the winter, the park's many hills offer wonderful tobogganing.

8: The family that plays together

As befits a city of its size and diversity, Toronto offers an inexhaustible range of leisure activities from hiking and biking to folk dancing and star-gazing — diversions that the entire family can enjoy. The following information is necessarily selective; be sure to check out the newspaper and other listings described in Chapter 1 for information on family activities week by week.

Biking

Toronto has several active bicycle advocacy groups that deserve credit for creating a bike-friendly city. Marked off-street bike paths run through several city parks; a few of the closest to downtown are the **David A. Balfour Park** at Mount Pleasant Road south of St. Clair Avenue; **Moore Park Ravine** on Moore Avenue west of Bayview Avenue; the **Lower Don parks system**, which includes a bike path that runs along the lower Don River and connects with the **Martin Goodman Trail** at its south end; and the trails running through the interconnected **Ernest Thompson Seton**, **Wilket Creek**, **Serena Gundy**, and **Sunnybrook parks** chain.

The **Martin Goodman Trail** is a 20-kilometre (12-mile) biking and jogging path that runs along the central waterfront from Balmy Beach in the east to the Humber River in the west. The **Bay Street Clearway**,

from the foot of Bay Street to north of Bloor Street, is a reserved lane for buses, taxis, and bikes between 7 am and 7 pm on weekdays. The **Leslie Street Spit**, also called Tommy Thompson Park (see page 142), offers a 5-kilometre (3-mile) flat road through an urban wilderness that attracts cyclists, strollers, and bird watchers on weekends. The other prime cycling spot is the **Toronto Islands** (see page 88), where you can ride from end to end without encountering any cars. On weekends, the ferries carry bikes only to Wards Island and Hanlan's Point; on weekdays, you can also take your bike on the Centre Island ferries. There is a bicycle rental kiosk on Centre Island. For hourly or daily bicycle rentals in the city, try **Wheel Excitement Inc.**, located near Harbourfront at 5 Rees Street (506-1001).

Helmets are essential for city cycling, and city by-laws discourage cycling on sidewalks, although the training-wheel set is tolerated. For more information on biking in Toronto, contact the City Cycling Committee (392-7592). Toronto celebrates cyclists during the annual Bike-to-Work Week, the third week in May, with free pancake breakfasts for cyclists at Nathan Phillips Square, organized rides, repair clinics, and concerts

147

performed by Toronto's one-of-a-kind Choir on Bikes. An excellent free pamphlet of bicycle route maps is available at **Sport Swap** cycling store, 2045 Yonge Street (481-0249). Or consult *The Great Toronto Cycling Guide*, by Elliot Katz, available at most bookstores.

Canoeing

Canoes are available on Centre Island at hourly rental rates for those interested in paddling the lazy waters of the

islands' lagoons. At Harbourfront, the **Harbourfront Canoe School** (203-2277) runs courses and workshops throughout the summer.

Fishing

The most popular spots for angling are **Grenadier Pond** in High Park, the trout pond at **Hanlan's Point** on the Toronto Islands, the mouth of the **Humber River** in the city's west end, and the **Scarborough Bluffs** beaches in the east end. The first two locations are recommended especially for children. Sad to say, however, the fish are just for catching, not eating: pollution has taken its unhealthy toll in Toronto's waters. Children under 18 do not require fishing licences, but if their adult companions intend to put in a line, they must first procure a licence from the provincial Ministry of Natural Resources (314-2000).

Fitness and gymnastics

The **Central YMCA** at 20 Grosvenor Street (2 blocks north of College Station) offers an inspiring array of fitness classes, sports activities, and weight-training equipment, and a snackbar for the health-conscious, all housed within an attractive, upscale building that has won several architectural awards.

Non-members can purchase a day pass, $13 for adults and $6 for children over six (children six and under are free), that will give them access to almost every feature, including two indoor pools.

The weekend-morning Kindergym classes provide young children with a workout in a closely supervised setting, while Mom and Dad can participate with them, attend an aerobics class, or play a few rounds of squash on their own. If you find yourself facing a rainy or snowy day, or if the kids need to burn off some excess energy, keep the Y in mind. Hourly babysitting services are available. Call 975-9622.

Folk and square dancing

There is open family folk dancing in **Winston Churchill Park** at St. Clair Avenue West and Spadina Road on Tuesday evenings in the summer. Kids are welcome and if they tire of dancing you can head over to the adjacent playground.

Sunday afternoons from September through March you can all dosido together at the Family Dance Party (square dancing and line dancing) held at the **Church of St. George the Martyr**, 195 John Street, with live callers and music; call 536-6362 for information on times and admission.

Golf

Metro Parks operates five public golf courses on a first-come, first-served basis. There are reduced greens fees for junior players. All courses are open from mid-April to late October. Call the course managers for more information.

Dentonia Park
East side of Victoria Park Avenue, just north of Danforth Avenue
392-2558

Don Valley
Yonge Street and William Carson Crescent, one stoplight south of Highway 401
392-2465

Humber Valley
Albion Road and Beattie Avenue, just north of Highway 401
392-2488

Scarlett Woods
Off Birchmount Avenue, north of Sheppard Avenue East

(just five minutes' drive from the Highway 401/Kennedy Road exit)

392-2484

Tam O'Shanter

Southwest corner of Jane Street and Eglinton Avenue West

392-2547

Horseback riding

Rouge Hill Riding Centre, 7420 Kingston Road (Highway 2 and Port Union Road), is the only stable within Metro's boundaries where riders can take a horse out for an hour and also receive instruction at an introductory level. The terrain through the Rouge River Valley is varied and as close to a wilderness area as can be found in Metro. Trail riders must be over nine years old, but there are pony rides for younger children. A one-hour supervised trail ride costs $14.95. There are staff on site with first-aid training and all trails are monitored with two-way radios. Call 284-6176 for hours and directions to stables.

Horse racing

Woodbine Racetrack, at Rexdale Boulevard and Highway 27 in Metro's north-west corner, is the place to catch thoroughbred horse races from May through late October. Call 675-6110 for race schedules and admission prices.

Ice skating

Many of the city's parks have outdoor artificial ice rinks that offer free skating from December through mid-March. Some that are centrally located and easily reached by public transit include the rinks in **Riverdale Park** (Broadview Avenue south of Danforth Avenue), **Withrow Park** (Logan Avenue south of Danforth Avenue), **Christie Pits** (Bloor and Christie Streets), and **Ramsden Park** (on Yonge Street opposite Rosedale Station).

For value-added skating, try **Nathan Phillips Square** at City Hall; skate rentals,

snackbar, and washrooms on site. **Harbourfront** has the world's largest outdoor artificial rink and offers a snackbar and cocktail bar on site, all with great lake views. Or visit **Hazelton Lanes**, the tony midtown shopping complex at Avenue Road and Yorkville Avenue. Parents can sip cappuccino and nibble biscotti inside while watching the youngsters skate on a charming small rink in the mall's central courtyard.

In-line skating

While in-line skaters with a death wish happily career along city streets, you might prefer to skate in the safer confines of the **Martin Goodman Trail**, especially that portion running through the eastern Beaches, or along any of the bike paths in the parks. You can rent skates at **Wheel Excitement Inc.** (506-1001) near Harbourfront, right on the Martin Goodman Trail. A downtown Rollerblading and skateboarding surface has been set up at Wellesley and Bay Streets, on the site of what was to have been the city's new ballet-opera house. You can rent skates at the on-site booth.

Kite flying

Toronto's Kitefliers club usually meets on Sunday afternoons in **Humber Bay Park** at the foot of Park Lawn Road in the city's west end. **Riverdale Park** (southwest of Broadview and Danforth Avenues) and the city's beaches are also popular spots for kite flying. You can choose from a range of fancy and not-so-fancy kites at **Touch the Sky** (203-0578) in the Queen's Quay Terminal at Harbourfront.

Model railroading

The **Model Railroad Club of Toronto**, 37 Hanna Avenue, which has been operating since the 1930s, welcomes visitors on the first Wednesday evening of every month. This is your chance to see Canada's largest model railway, with over 1500 metres (5000 feet) of track, 500 freight cars, 80 passenger cars, and 15 steam and 25 diesel engines, and to admire the intricate miniature world created by dedicated rail enthusiasts. The club also opens its doors for the annual "Romance of the Rails Show" on the last three Sundays in February. For more information on the club call 536-8927.

Radio-control flying

The sport flying of radio-controlled model airplanes is practised year-round at the **Humber Valley Field**, just north of Kipling and Steeles Avenues, in Metro's northwest end. The **Humber Valley R.C. Flyers Inc.**, who fly out of this field, can be reached at 616-3208.

Skiing and snowboarding

Downhill

The largest facility for downhill skiing within Metro is at the **North York Ski Centre** in Earl Bales Park at Bathurst Street and Sheppard Avenue. The ski centre has three intermediate slopes and one beginner slope, one double chair lift, one T-bar, and one rope tow. The slopes are professionally patrolled and there is lighting for night skiing. Equipment rentals are available. The centre is open from mid-December to mid-March and offers individual and family season passes. Daily rates range from $5 to $8 per hour, depending on the number of hours. Children four and younger ski free using the rope tow. The centre also offers courses in skiing and snowboarding. Call 395-7934 for snow conditions; 395-7874 for all other information.

Cross-country

Cross-country skiing is popular at **High Park**, on the **Toronto Islands**, and through the **Central Don Parks**. At the **Metro Zoo** skiers can enjoy viewing Canada's winter mammals in a natural snowy habitat (this beats seeing the Arctic wolves with their tongues hanging out on a hot day in August); call the Metro Zoo (392-5900) for information on hours and equipment rental charges.

Star-gazing

David Dunlop Observatory in Richmond Hill, just north of Metro, schedules public tours on Saturday evenings (times vary), which allow visitors to look through one of Canada's largest astronomical telescopes. No children under seven are admitted. Tour reservations are required three weeks in advance; call 905-884-2112.

Storytelling

If you and the older kids in your family have a shared

love of the spoken word, then you'll be enthralled by the tales at the weekly Friday-night storytelling sessions sponsored by the **Storytellers School of Toronto**. Their gatherings are held at 8:30 pm at the **Church of St. George the Martyr**, 195 John Street, just behind Grange Park; $3 for admission. The school operates several courses for aspiring storytellers, including one aimed at telling stories to young children. It also hosts the **Annual Toronto Festival of Storytelling**, on the last weekend in February, which attracts tellers and listeners from near and far; call 924-8625.

Swimming

Beaches

Notwithstanding its numerous beaches, Toronto is no Sydney, Australia. Lake Ontario's water is usually cold throughout the summer, and the beaches, which are monitored by the city's public health department, are often posted with no-swimming signs owing to pollution. Those brave enough to try the water can call the **Beaches Hotline** (392-7161) for the names of beaches listed as

Kidsummer

Kidsummer is a two-month schedule of free events for children aged four to twelve. To encourage kids to explore the city, there is an activity at a different site every day. Participants might go behind the scenes at a candy factory, watch a rehearsal of the National Ballet, or join in some games at a beach picnic. Kidsummer runs from July 1 through to the first Saturday in September. *Toronto Life* magazine publishes a calendar of the events in its July issue. Some events require preregistration; sign-up cards are available in the magazine or they may be picked up at participating sponsors. Call 364-3333 for more information on how to register. Throughout July and August, Kidsummer events are announced several times daily on CHFI FM98 radio and on the CBC TV News at 6 pm.

safe for swimming that day. Parents should be aware, however, that young children could be more susceptible than adults to the bacteria in the water. As a general rule, Toronto's eastern beaches are cleanest. These include the entire beachfront along **the boardwalk** south of Queen Street and east of Woodbine Avenue; **Ashbridge's Bay** at Coxwell Avenue and Lakeshore Boulevard East; and **Cherry Beach** at the foot of Cherry Street. The latter is a personal favourite, as it is seldom crowded and has a large parking lot. Cherry Beach features a washroom, picnic tables and hibachis, lots of windsurfers to watch, and usually a chip wagon where you can buy deliciously greasy fries to share with the seagulls. The beaches along the southern side of the Toronto Islands are very popular with families. If you want additional amenities like changerooms and snackbars, stick to **Centre Island**; if you're looking for a more secluded, natural type of beach, head for **Wards Island** or **Hanlan's Point**.

Pools

During the summer, the city's Parks and Recreation Department operates 12 outdoor pools with lockers, changerooms, and free admission. There's **Donald D. Summerville Olympic Pool** at Woodbine

Beach, and pools at **Riverdale Park** (Broadview and Danforth Avenues), **High Park** (Bloor and Keele Streets), and **Eglinton Park** (Eglinton Avenue and Avenue Road).

Swimming mixes with local history at the **Gus Ryder Pool** at Sunnyside Beach. Once part of a 6-hectare (15-acre) amusement complex, this pool is still popular with Toronto's west-enders. Opened in 1922, Sunny-side Amusement Park closed in the mid-1950s, after a sad descent into tackiness. The only remnants of Sunnyside's former glory are its pool, the grandiose bathing pavilion, and the Palais Royale dance hall.

Many of the city's parks have wading pools that are open in July and August. Indoor swimming is free year-round at numerous community centres and some schools; call Toronto Parks and Recreation at 392-1111 during business hours for more information.

Tennis

There are tennis courts open to the public free of charge in many of the city's parks. Some may be booked at certain hours by tennis clubs, but usually there will be an open court for public use by the half-hour. Just hang up your racquet on the board to reserve a court, and wait your turn. Two courts close to downtown and the TTC are at **Ramsden Park** (opposite Rosedale Station) and **Riverdale Park** (south of Broadview Station). To find other courts close to you, call Toronto Parks and Recreation at 392-1111.

Windsurfing

Wind Promotions (698-8933), located behind Donald D. Summerville Olympic Pool at **Woodbine Beach**, operates a school that offers windsurfing lessons for kids over 29.5 kilograms (65 pounds), $35 per two-hour session. They also rent boards for $10–$15 per hour for use at Woodbine Beach. The most popular spot to take your own board is **Cherry Beach**, at the foot of Cherry Street.

Amusement parks

Paramount Canada's Wonderland, see page 81.
Centreville, Toronto Islands, see page 89.
Ontario Place, see page 75.

Wild Water Kingdom

Where? 7855 Finch Avenue West, Brampton
369-WILD

TTC: From Finch Station take the Finch bus west, or from Yorkdale Station take the GO bus

When? June through September 10 am–8 pm

How much? Day pass for unlimited use of all water attractions: $15.88 for ages 10 and up, $12.15 for children 4–9, children under 4 free; after 4 pm, $9.35 rate for all ages; additional charges for mini-golf, batting cages, racetrack, and optional tube rentals

Extras: Parking $4.75 per day

Canada's largest water park is located just west of Metro and offers an array of water attractions, including a 1.2-hectare (half-acre) heated wave pool with 1.4-metre (4.5-foot) crashing waves and a surrounding "beach" of Astroturf; two seven-storey heated serpentine speed slides and eight other slides; and three body flumes. If all of this sounds a little too adventurous, there are also whirlpool tubs and a Lazy River floating tube ride. Younger children can let loose at the Dolphin Bay water playground with its tamer versions of the water slides and flumes. For landlubbers, the kingdom provides volleyball

French-language services

If you are a French-speaking family, or if your children are in French immersion programs at school, you may enjoy participating in some of the city's amenities *en français*.

Centre francophone de Toronto

20 Lower Spadina Avenue 203-1220

This is the main information service for French-speaking residents, newcomers, and visitors. The centre has a gallery that sponsors art exhibitions and concerts by francophone artists. A summary of the week's activities is published in the French-language weekly newspaper, *L'Express de Toronto*. Staff are *enchanté* to provide information on French cultural events, community and social services, and bookstores.

L'Express de Toronto

17 Carlaw Avenue 465-2107

This weekly newspaper, published on Wednesdays, has its finger on the pulse of the city's francophone community, which numbers about 50,000 native speakers and another 200,000 who speak French as a second language. Single copies are $1 and are available from larger news agents like Lichtman's and from French-language bookstores; a yearly subscription costs $40.

Bookstores

Toronto's three largest French-language bookstores are **La Maison de la Presse Internationale,** 124 Yorkville Avenue (928-0418), which offers a huge range of international French-language newspapers and magazines, other European magazines, and a book department with some children's titles; **Librairie Champlain,** 468 Queen Street East (364-4345), which stocks the largest selection of French books in the city; and the **Children's French Store,** 1486 Danforth Avenue (465-3015), which carries books and various educational products and is especially geared to students in immersion programs.

courts, baseball and soccer fields, batting cages, miniature golf, a remote-control car racetrack, and video games. There is a tree-lined beachside picnic area, a licensed patio barbecue restaurant, and various fast-food kiosks.

Indoor Playgrounds

Adventure Club

1520 Steeles Avenue West (just north of the city at Steeles Avenue and Dufferin Street)
905-669-PLAY

A 1,000-square-metre (11,000-square-foot) fitness-focused indoor playground, Adventure Club lets kids play all day for one low price (which reduces those "It's time to go" tantrums). The play area is fully supervised and offers state-of-the-art equipment: lots of windowed tunnels, an air-bouncer, ball baths, a trolley slide, and a craft corner. There is a separate area for children under three. Parents, who must remain on the premises, can take a break in the lounge, where movies are shown and food is available. All-day passes: $6.95 for children four to twelve years, $3.95 for children three and under, accompanying adults are free.

Woodbine Centre Fantasy Fair

Highway 27 and Rexdale Boulevard (in Metro's northwest end)
674-5200

Located in a large mall, Fantasy Fair bills itself as "Ontario's only indoor amusement park." It boasts eight full-size amusement rides, including a Ferris wheel, a merry-go-round, a haunted tunnel, and a large play area with a ball bath. Overall this is a reasonably priced outing if you're willing to make the trek, and you can combine a visit with some shopping. Ride tickets are 75¢ each, $19.95 for 30 tickets; all-day passes cost $9.95 for kids over 137 centimetres (54 inches), $7.95 for kids under 137 centimetres (54 inches). After 5 pm every day, kids can take unlimited rides for only $5.

Storefront pay-as-you-play playgrounds

For young children, toddlers to age six, these small storefront playgrounds can be the answer to a prayer on a blustery or rainy day. Some parents may feel a niggling guilt at the idea of paying to play, but if your conscience and your pocket-book allow, spend a few bucks for an hour's relief from cabin fever, a "free" cup of coffee, and the chance to commiserate with others in the same boat. After all, you're providing the kids with a "positive socialization experience." The indoor playgrounds are usually stocked with lots of big-ticket Fisher-Price, Playskool, and Little Tikes products, along with various other toys and perhaps some craft supplies. Parents must remain on the premises and supervise their kids: these places are not intended to be a substitute for babysitting services.

Giraffe's Playground
1A Hannaford Street
691-2941

This playground has a ball bath, climbing equipment, riding cars, slides, a playhouse, and a wide range of quality toys. Rates are $5 per family for the first hour; $1.50 per additional half-hour.

Kiddaroo Playground
1560 Bayview Avenue, Suite 202
489-6036

At Kiddaroo your kids will enjoy a large, bright room stocked with climbers, slides, and lots of let's-pretend items like a play kitchen and tool shop. For parents, there's a pleasant corner with magazines and unlimited coffee. Rates are $8 per hour per family for the first hour, with discounts for subsequent hours.

Kids Are Us
1107 Queen Street East
406-6759

If you feel comfortable dropping your kids off at a storefront playground, try this childcare business operated by a mother-and-daughter team who welcome kids from infants up to age eight. See page 39 for hours and rates.

L'il Monkeys' Playground
3300 Yonge Street
487-3189

Facilities include a ball house and lots of climbing equipment. Rates are $5 per hour for one child, $8 per hour for more than one child; $1 per hour thereafter.

9: A city of neighbourhoods

Toronto prides itself on the distinctiveness of its many neighbour- hoods, the names of which reflect the city's history and the diverse ethnic communities that live here. Once your family has seen the major sights of the downtown core, venture off the beaten track and sample the unique delights of the Annex, Greektown on the Danforth, Chinatown, Little Italy, Kensington Market, Little India, or the Beaches. These areas have a personality all their own and make Toronto one of the most cosmopolitan cities in the world.

The neighbourhood walking tours described here have been kept short and simple, with the understanding that many kids will flag on long treks. Wherever possible, I've included directions to the clos- est park or outdoor spot where adults can take a breather and the kids can play.

The durations recommended for each walk reflect the average length of time a family would likely need to complete the outing, including a break for a snack or quick meal. The recommendations don't include any time for visiting the highlighted attractions along the way. The restaurants

1	BCE Place	8	Toronto Sculpture Garden
2	Hockey Hall of Fame	9	St. James Cathedral
3	O'Keefe Centre,	10	St. Lawrence Neighbourhood
	St. Lawrence Centre		and playgrounds
4	Gooderham Flatiron Bldg		
5	Market Square		**TTC Stations**
6	St. Lawrence Market	A	Queen
	(South Bldg)	B	King
7	St. Lawrence Hall	C	Union

and refuelling stops have been chosen for their reasonable prices, efficient service, special kid-food appeal, and convenient location along the route.

You may want to bring a detailed map of the city on your walk. This chapter's tour maps include main streets only.

Walk #1 Downtown East

Where? Between King and Front Streets, east of Bay Street

Start: At BCE Place, 181 Bay Street

Finish: St. James Cathedral,

161

at King and Church Streets
How long? 2 to 3 hours

Your starting point for this walk is **BCE Place**, the lofty skyscraper with an entrance on Bay Street, just north of Front

Street. Walk through the remarkable galleria to the preserved back wall of the old Bank of Montreal Building (1888), which has been incorporated into BCE Place and now houses part of the **Hockey Hall of Fame** (see page 111). Pass through the central concourse of BCE Place and exit onto Yonge Street just a few steps north of Front Street. As you go east along Front, you'll see two of the city's largest theatres, the **O'Keefe Centre** and the **St. Lawrence Centre for the Arts**. If you are visiting at Christmas, the O'Keefe is sure to be full of young balletomanes enjoying one of Toronto's longest-running theatrical traditions, the National Ballet of Canada's

The Nutcracker. At other times of the year, the 3200-seat O'Keefe often features dance companies, large musicals, or big-name kids' shows like *Sesame Street Live* that make for an entertaining family occasion. Call 393-7469 for box office information.

The south-side stretch of Front Street East between Scott and Church Streets is best appreciated from **Berczy Park**, the small square of green space behind the landmark **Gooderham Building** (1892), Toronto's own Flatiron. From here you can admire the ornate elegance of the facades of the renovated late-19th-century warehouses that line Front Street, while kids get a kick out of the eye-tricking, multi-storey mural on the Gooderham's west wall. The street-level shops that now occupy these former warehouses are a browser's paradise. First among them is **Nicholas Hoare**, doubtless Toronto's most gorgeously appointed bookstore. Done up to resemble a turn-of-the-century London bookshop, Nicholas Hoare thrills the bibliophile with its enormous selection of titles ranged along oak shelves with gleaming brass rails. Sliding book ladders allow access to the top shelves, and there is a large tiled fireplace and comfy couches for relaxing while you peruse your choices. Young customers enjoy the same elegant treatment at the back of the store, where they can curl up in tiny Regency-striped wing chairs and lose themselves in the land of *Where the Wild Things Are* or *Through the Looking Glass.*

In the same block, don't miss **Flatiron's Department Store**, at no. 51, a bulging-at-the-seams emporium of toys, gifts, and quality *tchotchkes*

from around the world. Flatiron's biggest attraction is its huge backroom stuffed year-round with every imaginable Christmas accoutrement. There are thousands of tree decorations, crèche sets, figurines, candles, music boxes, and other seasonal gewgaws.

When you reach Church Street, cross over to the north side of Front Street and continue east to **Market Square**, a luxury condominium complex that houses a handful of shops and restaurants and a multi-screen movie theatre. If the weather's unaccommodating, this is a good place to take shelter and have a cup of coffee at **Café Coco**, at the complex's east end. Before you head inside, though, pause to take a look at one of Toronto's best views, that of **St. James Cathedral** framed by the courtyard and the gates of Market Square as you look north between the complex's two wings. This is a photo-op that shouldn't be missed.

Exiting Market Square at the east end, you'll arrive at one of Toronto's few piazzas, the bricked courtyard between Market Square and the north

building of the **St. Lawrence Market**. On weekends, when the market is bustling, this square, also called **Market Park**, is full of buskers and street merchants — not to mention well-fed pigeons.

Shopping at St. Lawrence Market is an enduring Toronto tradition. The South Market is open six days a week (closed on Sundays), but Saturday is the day for chance encounters with friends and acquaintances. There's action on all three floors of this restored 1844 building, which was originally Toronto's first city hall. The basement and street level house butchers and bakers, fishmongers and greengrocers. If you want to make like a local at the market, munch a bacon-on-a-bun sandwich as you walk about; these are a specialty of the delis on the main floor. After cruising the aisles of these two floors — a treat for all the senses — enjoy an overview of the South Market from the second-storey **Market Gallery**, which displays photography and art that portray the city's past (see page 120).

Across Front Street the North Market building hosts a farmers' market on Saturdays only, when southern Ontario farmers truck in their wares and set up their stalls before 5 am. Here you can find sausages and to-die-for pies and jams that originate in the Mennonite country near Kitchener-Waterloo. All of the produce is fresh-picked and there's nary a scrap of plastic wrap in sight.

From the market, head north on Jarvis Street to King Street, where you'll come across another of Toronto's "old" city halls, the perfectly proportioned **St. Lawrence Hall** (1850) at 157 King Street East. This Victorian gem has also doubled as a performance site and rehearsal hall for the National Ballet of Canada. A few doors west on King Street is one of the city's most unusual public spaces, the **Toronto Sculpture Garden**, which displays large-scale contemporary works in a small park that is bordered on one side by a wall of falling water. Kids often respond enthusiastically to the built-in whimsy of these avant-garde installations. Gardens of a more traditional sort are to be found across King Street, east of **St. James Cathedral** (1853). Their picturesque formality may make you want to stroll around in long skirts with a parasol, so authentic is their intended 19th-century feel. If you can persuade the young ones to take a peek inside the cathedral, you'll find an excellent example of Gothic architecture, executed with Canadian restraint. The cathedral's spire, measuring 99 metres (324 feet), is the tallest in the country.

To find playgrounds in the St. Lawrence Market area,

walk south on Jarvis Street to The Esplanade, then continue east. This puts you in the thick of the St. Lawrence Neighbourhood, a model redevelopment project that created a vibrant community in an area that was once dominated by run-down factories and abandoned warehouses. All along The Esplanade there is a chain of parks, playgrounds, and fountains that serve the 10,000 neighbourhood residents and provide the area with a friendly and welcoming atmosphere.

On The Esplanade between Scott and Church Streets is where you'll find the **Organ Grinder** and the **Old Spaghetti Factory** restaurants, both catering to families with inexpensive and predictable pasta and pizza entrees. The Organ Grinder is often used for birthday parties, and has lots of video games and amusements, not to mention the rebuilt century-old pipe organ that gives the restaurant its name. If you are in search of more interesting food possibilities, check out **Pizzeria Uno**, at 73 Front Street East, which has a large gourmet-style pizza menu with a $3.95 kids' special; the venerable **Shopsy's Delicatessen**,

165

33 Yonge Street, with its array of blintzes and latkes and other deli treats; and **Gert's**, 100 Front Street East, a casual cafeteria with some of the best home-made soups in the city.

If you crave variety and don't mind the complicated logistics of visiting a variety of food stations to fetch your own meal, then the **Mövenpick Marché** restaurant, in BCE Place, is worth a visit. A foodies' Disneyland, the Marché offers a huge array of well-priced choices prepared at "market stands" throughout the large, exuberantly decorated restaurant. It's your job to navigate through the food options — tray in hand — selecting as you go. Nothing's quite gourmet-level, but it's all tasty: everything from Thai noodles to spaghetti bolognese, from rösti (yummy diced and fried Swiss potatoes) with sautéed veal to fruit salad with muesli. The baked goods are generally excellent, the bowls of café au lait are generous. It can be an effort, however, to get everyone's meal to the table; if you're on your own with young kids, this restaurant is not recommended. But with two adults to coordinate your team, the Marché is an entertaining dining experience and kids love it.

Walk #2 Downtown West

Where? Between Queen and Front Streets, west of Bay Street
Start: Toronto City Hall
Finish: Toronto City Hall
How long? 2$\frac{1}{2}$ to 3$\frac{1}{2}$ hours

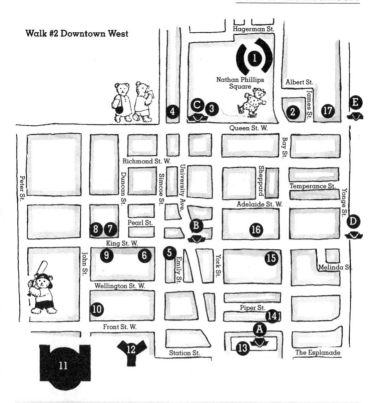

Walk #2 Downtown West

1	Toronto City Hall	12	CN Tower
2	Old City Hall	13	Union Station
3	Osgoode Hall	14	Royal Bank Plaza
4	Campbell House	15	Toronto-Dominion Centre
5	St. Andrew's Church	16	First Canadian Place
6	Roy Thomson Hall	17	Eaton Centre
7	Royal Alexandra Theatre		
8	Princess of Wales Theatre	**TTC**	
9	Metro Hall	A Union	D King
10	CBC Broadcasting Centre	B St. Andrew	E Queen
11	SkyDome	C Osgoode	

The obvious spot to begin a tour of the western core of downtown is **Toronto City Hall**, at Bay and Queen Streets. Take a few minutes to admire the Romanesque extravaganza of Old City Hall, on the east side of Bay Street, whose delightfully mocking gargoyles will arouse a few giggles from the kids. The building that Torontonians still sometimes call "new" City Hall is one of Metro's most prominent landmarks and has become a true focal point for community

167

activity and entertainment (see page 64 for a description of year-round events). You can take a self-guided tour of the building; just pick up a brochure at the reception desk in the foyer. Skating on the artificial rink in Nathan Phillips Square is a popular local tradition and it's fun to see the odd business type from a nearby bank tower blading by on his or her lunch hour (skate rentals available).

Next door to City Hall is **Osgoode Hall** (constructed between 1832 and 1846, with numerous later additions), bastion of the Supreme Court of Ontario and home to the Law Society of Upper Canada, the legal profession's provincial regulating body. Tours are offered during the summer months, taking visitors behind the scenes to areas of the building not normally open to the public.

Osgoode Hall is perhaps best known to locals for its "cow gate" — a wrought-iron configuration designed to keep out the stray cattle that were apparently a neighbourhood nuisance back in 1866. Other features worth noting are the bullet holes in the second-floor

courtroom that date from a notorious 1986 attack during a trial; the refurbished 1860s-style courtroom; and the awe-inspiring Great Library with its wonderful twisting staircase, imposing fireplace, and intricately patterned ceiling. The tour will also take you to the small museum of the Law Society of Upper Canada. This is likely a site of somewhat specialized interest for older kids who might have a lawyer

in the family or who have legal — or criminal — aspirations of their own. Strollers are welcome on the tour, but some areas may be inaccessible.

Osgoode Hall
Where? 116–138 Queen Street West
947-3300
TTC: At Osgoode Station
When? Weekday tours (suitable for children 10

Still in the legal vein is **Campbell House**, at the northwest corner of Queen Street and University Avenue, built for a distinguished judge in 1822 and operating today as headquarters for the Advocates Society and as a museum. Call 597-0227 for information on tours of the house and on special family programming that takes place on holidays throughout the year.

Continuing west along Queen Street, turn south at Simcoe Street, and head down to King Street. At the corner of King and Simcoe, pause to admire both the 19th-century solidity of **St. Andrew's Presbyterian Church** (1874) and the airy modernism of **Roy Thomson Hall**, home of the Toronto Symphony Orchestra and the city's prime musical venue. RTH conducts regular tours (see page 128) and its shop is not to be missed if you have music lovers on your gift list. Across from RTH is the King Street theatre district, home of the venerable **Royal Alexandra Theatre** (1906) and the recently built **Princess of Wales Theatre**.

Metro Hall, just west of Roy Thomson, is the seat of government of Metropolitan Toronto and the scene of various civic celebrations during the year. Don't miss the outdoor sculpture on the south side of Metro

169

Hall: kids love to speculate on what all those dog-like creatures are howling at.

South of Metro Hall is the **CBC Broadcasting Centre**, the recently opened headquarters of the Canadian Broadcasting Corporation, at 250 Front Street West. This new building brought together all the diverse operations of the corporation that until 1992 had been scattered in various run-down fire-traps around the city. The building is constructed around a large central atrium, and if you visit the ground floor you might spot some of those "national faces" from your TV screen. It's also possible to watch a live local radio broadcast in progress through the main-floor studio windows, between 6 and 9 am, 12 and 2 pm, and 4 and 6 pm.

Weekday guided tours take visitors into studios and newsrooms — but only when these are not in use. Kids have a chance to see some of the technology and equipment, and learn interesting facts and trivia from the tour escort. A visit to the **CBC Museum** (open Monday–Friday 10 am–4 pm), complete with costumes, old microphones, archival footage, and other memorabilia, rounds out the tour. An annual open house, with lots of celebs and kids' activities, is usually held during Toronto Artsweek, the last week in September.

The **Glenn Gould Studio** frequently hosts noon-time and other music concerts, some of them free. If these interest your family, call the studio box office at 205-5555. If you want to attend a Thursday-night taping of the "Royal Canadian Air Farce" TV show, call 205-5050 to arrange for free tickets.

The CBC Broadcasting Centre

Where? 250 Front Street West 205-8605 for tour reservations
TTC: From Union Station walk west along Front Street
When: Usually daily Mondays–Fridays, but call to confirm times; preregistration required
How much? Free
How long? Tours are 45 minutes

At the foot of John Street is the massive white clam shell of **SkyDome**, Toronto's sports shrine and home to the Blue Jays (American League baseball team), the Argonauts (Canadian Football League team), and the newest gang on the block, the Raptors (National Basketball Association team) — pending the construction of the basketball team's new facility. SkyDome also provides a venue for numerous concerts, trade shows, and special events year-round.

An engineering marvel that opened its doors in 1989, SkyDome is the world's first domed stadium with a fully retractable roof. The four-sectioned roof is built on rails that allow it to be closed in just 20 minutes, and if you're lucky enough to be at a game when the roof is being opened or closed, you could miss a home run; like everyone else in the 50,000-plus seats, your attention will be focused on the drama overhead.

SkyDome offers public tours that are well worth taking, especially for the keen sports fans in the family. Visitors see such behind-the-scenes features as the visiting-team dressing room, the media centre, and one of the private corporate SkyBoxes, which were sold for between $1 and $2 million when the stadium opened — per square foot, they're probably Toronto's most expensive real estate. For youngsters, the biggest thrill is sitting in the team dugouts and walking out on the huge Astroturf field. They might even have a chance to stand on the hydraulic pitcher's mound.

If you are attending a game with little ones, keep in mind the small indoor playground

on the first level near section 115 for moments when the kids get restless. There are numerous McDonald's outlets in SkyDome, and a large restaurant on the east side, but be forewarned that the prices here are significantly higher than at regular McDonald's locations.

SkyDome
Where? Front and John Streets, just west of the CN Tower
341-2770 for tours and event information
TTC: From Union Station walk west along Front Street or use the SkyWalk from the upper level of the railway station, or take the King streetcar to John Street and walk south

When? Tours usually operate between 10 am and 4 pm on days when there is no scheduled event or game
How much? $9 for adults, $6 for children under 16, children 3 and under free
How long? Tour is 45 minutes long, after a 15-minute film on SkyDome's construction
Extras: Not stroller or wheelchair accessible for tours, discounted parking available in the SkyDome lot at the west end of the stadium on non-event days

Leaving SkyDome, you have the option of visiting the **CN Tower** (see page 66) before entering the enclosed and elevated **SkyWalk** that will take you back to **Union Station** at Front and Bay Streets. It's worth taking a peek at the station for its impressive 260-metre-long (850-foot) colonnaded facade and its massive, vaulted foyer — tangible reminders of the romantic Age of Rail and the crucial role that railways played in Canada's development. Unfortunately, kids can't actually see trains up close while they are in the station; but they can get a great aerial view from the glassed-in

Toronto's downtown walkway

Toronto's frequently inclement winters led to the creation of a 10-kilometre (6-mile) network of underground walkways that connect most of the major downtown office buildings to each other and to the subway system.

Some Torontonians who live in high-rise buildings over subway stations and work in downtown towers pride themselves on never stepping outside from December through April: they can live, eat, work, shop, and go to the movies without a hint of winter's icy blasts.

If you are setting out to navigate the walkway, it's

handy to have a map, which you can pick up in one of many receptacles en route. The system of direction signs that run through the concourses is called **PATH**. Although the signs are intended to reduce confusion,
most newcomers find the labyrinth a bit intimidating.

If you enter the walkway at the south end (Union Station), you can go north all the way to the Coach Terminal at Bay and Dundas Streets.

Along the route, you'll pass through some prime shopping concourses under the Royal Bank Plaza, Toronto-Dominion Centre, Scotia Plaza, and First Canadian Place — hundreds of stores of every kind. You can check out the Hockey Hall of Fame, enjoy a concert at Roy Thomson Hall, or take in a movie at the Sheraton Centre or the Eaton Centre.

Because the shopping concourses around King and Bay Streets cater chiefly to the business crowd, they are usually deserted on Saturdays and can be great places to browse on nasty days.

Stroller-pushing parents find the ease of having so many stores in one place without the hassle of curbs and steps a great boon year-round.

SkyWalk. Youngsters love to feel the trains rumble underneath their feet as they look down over a weaving network of tracks leading into the country's largest railway station.

Across from Union Station are the dazzling towers of the **Royal Bank Plaza**, whose windows, in an extravagant display of 1970s affluence and confidence, were actually coated with real gold. Go north on Bay to Wellington Street and turn left: half a block along you'll discover Toronto's most kid-appealing outdoor work of art, Saskatchewan artist Joe Fafard's deliciously indolent life-size bronze cows. Entitled **"The Pasture,"** the cattle recline peacefully on the lawn of the IBM Tower, which is part of the rigorously modern Toronto-Dominion Centre complex. Although they are sometimes roped off, the cows are irresistible to kids: mine love to race around them and play hide-and-seek, while I simply find their pastoral stillness to have a magically calming effect in the middle of the nation's busiest financial district.

One of the best high-altitude views of the city can be had for free at the top of the **Toronto-Dominion Bank Tower**. Ride the elevator to the 55th floor and enter the foyer of the Cadillac Fairview Corporation offices. The staff here are happy to let you look down over the waterfront, using their mounted, high-power binoculars. If the CN Tower prices are out of your league, head for the TD Centre.

Just a block farther west along King Street, on the north side, is the **Exchange Tower** at **First Canadian Place**, the Bank of Montreal's entry into Toronto's build-a-higher-skyscraper contest. Here you can take a free tour of the **Toronto Stock Exchange**, one of North America's largest stock exchanges, which handles about 75 percent of the total value of trading in Canada. From the public viewing gallery overlooking the trading floor, you can watch all those puts and calls being carried out by the often frenzied traders. Older children and teens can be introduced to the basics of the capitalist economy through a 45-minute presentation offered by the TSE. The exchange also gives out educational materials about its history and how the stock market works.

Toronto Stock Exchange

Where? 2 First Canadian Place, Exchange Tower at King and York Streets 947-4676 for tour information
TTC: From St. Andrew Station walk east to York Street
When? Public gallery open Monday–Friday 9 am–4:30 pm, presentations Tuesdays–Fridays at 2 pm
How much? Free

From the Exchange Tower, walk north up York Street and you'll find yourself back at City Hall, where everyone can cool their toes in the Nathan Phillips Square fountain.

Your choices of places to eat in the downtown core are almost infinite. For easy snacking, head underground to the numerous shopping concourses beneath the bank buildings, all of which have food courts. The one under First Canadian Place offers an enticing choice of fresh- and fast-food outlets with an international twist. If the weather is cooperative, grab a hot dog and some chunky home fries from the cart and truck vendors by City Hall. For sit-down restaurant eating

with something special for the kids, try **Wayne Gretzky's**, 99 Blue Jays Way, just north of the Dome. Young hockey fans can choose from a standard kids' menu (grilled cheese, burgers, pizza, macaroni) for between $2.99 and $3.99 while basking in the glory of the Great One's memorabilia. The various restaurants operated by millionaire retailer and arts patron Honest Ed Mirvish — **Ed's Warehouse**, **Ed's Italian**, **Ed's Chinese**, and **Ed's Seafood** — all offer reliable, reasonably priced menus and lots of eye-catching decor. You'll find them on King Street at the corner of Duncan, across from Metro Hall.

Walk # 3
The Beaches

Where? Queen Street East, east of Woodbine Avenue to Victoria Park Avenue
Start: Queen Street East and Woodbine Avenue
Finish: Queen Street East and Glen Manor Drive, or continue east to Nursewood Road for the Filtration Plant
How long? 2 to 4 hours

The Beaches is Toronto's premier neighbourhood for families out for a weekend stroll. Bounded by Lake Ontario and the boardwalk on the south, and Queen Street on the north, the Beaches has the feel of a small-town community. The residents here have a relaxed air and there is even an haute-casual Beaches style of dress: the locals look as if they might just as easily be cruising the boardwalk at Santa Cruz as promenading in conservative Toronto.

Allow several hours for a Beaches outing. Queen East boasts a wide range of restaurants, outdoor patios, pubs, bakeries and delis, toy stores, bookstores, children's clothing stores, specialty shops, and parks, and an excellent public library. When you have had enough boulevarding, you can always head down a sidestreet to the boardwalk and build a few sandcastles on the beach or skip stones in the lake. See page 134 for a complete description of the Beaches lakefront parks.

If you are planning a weekend jaunt to the Beaches, be warned that in good weather the parking scene can be horrific. There are no parking garages along Queen East to spoil the neighbourhood feel (there are a few lots north and south of Queen), but this means that the sidestreets are jammed. Queen East itself is slow and just about comes to a stop on a sunny Saturday or Sunday. From downtown, you

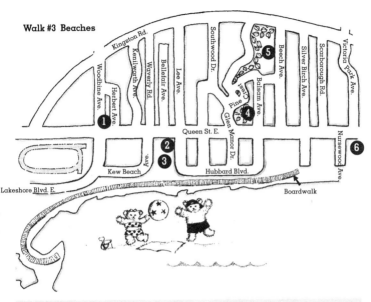

Walk #3 Beaches

1 Firehall	4 Ivan Forrest Gardens
2 Beaches Library	5 Glen Stewart Ravine
3 Kew Gardens	6 R.C. Harris Filtration Plant

are better off taking the Queen streetcar, for a pleasant 30-minute ride east to the Beaches (get off at Woodbine Avenue and walk east). You can also take the Bloor-Danforth subway east and hop a south-bound bus from Woodbine Station, then get off at Queen East.

Heading east from Woodbine, take a look at the fire station on the north side. With its picturesque tower and red brick exterior, it's typical of a style used for many firehalls throughout the city, and kids are always drawn to these castle-like buildings. The City of Toronto Fire Department has a policy of welcoming visitors to their stations (unless, of course, they are responding to an alarm), and often an on-duty firefighter is willing to show kids the inside of the station or the trucks. Naturally, these firehalls are open at any time of day, so feel free to drop in. See page 107 for information on the Toronto Fire Department.

If your kids are in need of a trim, try **Little Tots Hair Shop** at 1926 Queen East. No appointment necessary, just add your child's name to the list at the front desk, then send him or her to play in the ball bath at the rear of the store. The shop sells toys and novelty items, but the staff don't seem to mind if the young customers handle everything and buy nothing. The salon chairs are designed to resemble fun vehicles like fire engines and boats, and the stylists are experienced in dealing with even the most reluctant clients from toddlers on up. Haircuts are around $12 for kids; the staff will also do adult cuts for varying prices.

For a snack before or after your Little Tots visit, try the **Kew Beach Grill** next door at 1922 Queen East or **Aida's Falafel & Shish-Kabab** across the street at 1921 Queen East. The grill has a typical diner-style menu — the blueberry pancakes are a popular choice — and the waitresses here enjoy serving kids. If you are blessed with adventurous eaters, then don't hesitate to sample Aida's inexpensive Middle Eastern dishes; besides falafel, there's hummus, taboulleh, fried eggplant, lentil soup, and baclava for dessert. You order at the counter for eat-in or take-out and service is quick and pleasant. They'll happily provide a fresh warm pita for the picky eaters in your group.

Farther down the road, **Mastermind of the Beaches**, 1947 Queen East, is a quality toy store with a good assortment of brand names like Playmobil and Brio, and a strong selection of puzzles, computer games, and activity books for all ages.

Lick's Burger & Ice Cream at 1960 Queen East is a family mecca for burgers, hot dogs, chicken, fries, and ice cream. It's always busy and raucous, and most kids think it's awesome. Twenty-five flavours of ice cream and an impressive choice of shakes, sodas, and other frozen confections are a big draw during the summer. There is a play area upstairs for young children, affording their parents a chance to chill out over a coffee.

Another reliable spot is **Il Fornello** at 1968 Queen East. There's an eclectic menu of gourmet-style pizzas for grown-ups, or choose from the pasta selections or the daily lunch buffet. The kids' menu offers a choice of the buffet, a mini-pizza, or pasta, with pop and ice cream, for under $5. All ages will report satisfaction with this outlet of the successful Il Fornello chain.

While your kids might not always leap at the opportunity to visit an art gallery, they'll feel differently about the **World of Animation** at 1977 Queen East. This upstairs space sells original works by animation artists, including those from the Disney Studio. A visit here is a great way to help children appreciate the level of skill and artistry that goes into making cartoons.

Absolutely Diapers at 1984 Queen East is a veritable temple of diapers for the all-cloth set. They carry several brands of non-disposables and of diaper-wraps, along with clothing for babies and toddlers. If you're looking for the latest in diapering technology, this is definitely the place.

South of the intersection of Queen and Bellefair is **Kew Gardens**, one of the city's most pleasant parks, and the real hub of the neighbourhood for families with youngsters. There is an excellent playground, with a Buckminster Fuller-type geodesic rope climber and a wading pool. The park contains a bandstand that has evening concerts during the summer (call Toronto Parks and Recreation at 392-1111 for the schedule), tennis courts, a baseball diamond, and an artificial ice rink in the winter. Washrooms near the playground are open in the summer. The park is also home to the well-attended Beaches Jazz Festival in July.

At the northeast corner of Kew Gardens is the Beaches branch of the **Toronto Public Library**. This is a great place to find cover if the weather takes a turn. There's a large children's section downstairs, and lots of crannies for young readers to curl up in with a good book. Paper and crayons are always available. On most weekends there are scheduled kids' activities — crafts, movies, puppet shows — that are free and open to all children.

Toy Circus at 2036 Queen East is a well-stocked store, with many small items that parents can purchase cheaply as mementoes of the family's outing. Another local restaurant landmark is **Griffiths** at 2086 Queen East. Its Tudor-style, wood-panelled facade and windows full of butter tarts should make it irresistible. They serve an all-day breakfast and have a summer rooftop patio. **Comics Corner** at 2116C Queen East will appeal to older kids with its exhaustive stock of comic books and comic-book-character merchandise.

If you're feeling foot-weary, you can either end your walking tour or take a breather in the beautiful setting of the **Ivan Forrest Gardens**, at the corner of Queen and Glen Manor Drive. At the south end of this ravine park is a ravishing rock garden with a small waterfall: a few minutes here and you'll be recharged. Then, if you're up for a hike, head to the top end of the Glen Manor East Drive north until you see the sign for the **Glen Stewart Ravine** nature trail. This marked trail extends for half a kilometre (¼ mile) to Kingston Road and along it you can see several species of trees and a variety of plant life (look out for poison ivy). Up to 110 species of migrating birds have been spotted here in spring.

In the next block of Queen,

you'll find two storefronts that offer creative opportunities for kids: **Beadworks** at 2154 Queen East and **Kidz Creartive Playhouse** at 2156 Queen East. The former is a treasure trove of beads of all shapes and sizes for jewellery-making and other crafts, and they offer some workshops. The latter (that's "creartive" as in "art") is a craft centre, operated by a local mother, where you are free to drop in and participate in a craft activity with your child on a pay-as-you-play basis. The store offers scores of plaster moulds for painting, and lots of other supplies — and they do the clean-up. There is a backroom for birthday parties that can be fully managed by the store staff, who will handle everything from the invitations to the food.

Around ten blocks farther east, is the **R.C. Harris Filtration Plant**. This 1937 art deco building houses one of the city's main water treatment facilities, and is well worth a visit to view both its imposing architecture and its fascinating mechanics. Drawing in millions of litres daily from Lake Ontario through monstrous pipes, the plant treats the water in a variety of ways, all of which can be observed on weekend public tours that are guided by knowledgeable and enthusiastic employees. It's fun to pass through the long, labyrinthine corridors and passages of this huge plant; the spooky, dank atmosphere of the filter galleries, where water percolates through many layers of sand and gravel, is unique. Built in the golden era of public works, the plant is awash in marble, gilt, and mosaics, and has been used as a set for several films and the TV series "Robocop." It was also the scene of a memorable literary reading by international award-winning Toronto author Michael Ondaatje, who used the filtration plant as a setting in his novel *In the Skin of a Lion*.

R.C. Harris Filtration Plant

Where? 2701 Queen Street East at Nursewood Road 392-2932
TTC: Take the Queen streetcar east to Nursewood Road, the loop where the car makes the turn back along Queen East
When? Public tours on Saturdays and Sundays at 10 and 11:30 am, 1:30 and 3 pm
How much? Free
Extras: Great views of the Scarborough Bluffs and beaches from the extensive grounds

Walk #4 Bloor-Yorkville

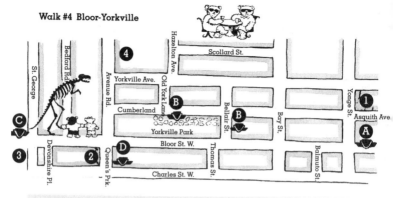

1 Metropolitan Toronto Reference Library	**TTC**
2 Royal Ontario Museum	A Bloor-Yonge
3 Bata Shoe Museum	B Bay (two exits)
4 Hazelton Lanes	C St. George
	D Museum

Walk #4 Bloor-Yorkville

Where? North of Bloor Street between Yonge Street and Avenue Road

Start: Bloor and Yonge Streets

Finish: Bloor Street and Avenue Road

How long? 2 to 3 hours

This midtown area is home to the city's chicest designer shops, and style is the watchword here, whether it's on the department-store scale of Holt Renfrew on Bloor Street, or in a tiny, exclusive Cumberland Street boutique. Many Torontonians love to stroll this mixed residential and commercial neighbourhood just for the fun of seeing and being seen. There's lots of opportunity for both at the numerous sidewalk cafés and curbside benches.

Despite its upscale aura, the Bloor-Yorkville area

offers lots for families of more modest means. Starting at the corner of Bloor and Yonge Streets — which self-absorbed Torontonians think of as the crossroads of Canada — head north on Yonge to the **Albert Britnell Book Shop**, 765 Yonge Street. Founded in 1893, this is one of the oldest bookstores in North America, and its selection of books, including children's titles, is always first-rate. Knowledgeable staff are happy to order any book that they can track down for you. Still in a bookish vein, the **Metropolitan Toronto Reference Library**, 789 Yonge Street, is well worth a visit for its architecture, by Raymond Moriyama, and for its uplifting ambiance. Built in 1977, it houses over 80 kilometres (50 miles) of shelves containing over 1.5 million books. For kids, the best part is a ride in the glassed-in elevator that glides up through the five-storey central atrium. Another highlight of the library is the Arthur Conan Doyle Room, a period-decorated room which is home to an extensive collection of Sherlock Holmes books and memorabilia.

Head west on Yorkville Avenue into the heart of

Yorkville Village. Many of the original village's Victorian homes have been preserved and now houses a mix of mostly expensive shops, galleries, and restaurants. On Saturdays through the fall, winter, and spring you're likely to happen upon an art show opening, with the artist in attendance. Most gallery owners are pleased to welcome families as long as the kids are well behaved, and an afternoon of gallery browsing makes for an inexpensive outing. You'll find most of the area's galleries on Hazelton Avenue and Scollard Street. If you head down the driveway at 37 Hazelton, you'll arrive at the open playing field attached to Jesse Ketchum School, which also has a playground and wading pool.

Back on Yorkville Avenue, the balletomanes in your group won't want to miss **Paper Things** at no. 99, the National Ballet's shop that sells all sorts of dance-related gifts, wrappings, cards, and knick-knacks. **Oh Yes Toronto**, at 101 Yorkville, sells T-shirts, sweatshirts, and children's clothes all emblazoned with Toronto landmarks and symbols — perfect gifts to take home with you. There are several children's clothing shops in the Yorkville area, all of them on the high-ticket side. One worth checking out is **Kid U Co**. at 9A Yorkville for its stock of Dr. Denton's, the legendary hard-wearing sleepers and other items that are hard to find elsewhere.

Once you have strolled the length of Yorkville Avenue to Avenue Road, circle back to Old York Lane, the passage-way that connects Yorkville Avenue to Cumberland Street. You'll emerge at the western end of **Yorkville Park**, an unconventional new park constructed over a subway station, whose unique design is intended to be "an unexpected and unusual demonstration of urban ecology and education, local history, and regional identity," according to the City's Parks and Recreation Department. Be that as it may, one feature of the park draws kids like a magnet: the mammoth outcropping of Canadian

Shield granite that rises majestically from the ground, close to the park's western end. Approximately one billion years old, and weighing 650 tonnes (715 tons), the Village Rock was taken from a farm property northeast of Gravenhurst, Ontario, transported on 20 flatbed trailers in 135 pieces, and reassembled at the park. It offers an irresistible surface for climbing and jumping, and adults can watch the kids scramble on the rock from the comfort of a bright red bistro-style chair, lulled by the soothing sounds of the Curtain of Water fountain adjoining the rock.

The rest of the park is also worth checking out. Overall there are 13 distinct areas, including plantings that evoke marshlands, orchards, herb gardens, prairie wildflower gardens, and alder and birch groves. At the eastern end there is a Scots pine grove where each tree is encircled by a pre-cast seating ring and light standards emit "a gentle fog that is supposed to simulate the early morning atmosphere of an evergreen forest" — I kid you not.

If you go south on Bellair Street, you'll come out on Bloor Street, right in the thick of Designers' Row, with shops like Chanel and Armani — a window shopper's paradise. You can stop your walking tour here or head over to the **Royal Ontario Museum** (page 84) at Avenue Road, or to the **Bata Shoe Museum** (page 94) at St. George Street. Or if you want to escape inclement weather, have a cappuccino or hot chocolate, and gaze in more fancy shop windows, head north on Avenue Road to the **Hazelton Lanes** shopping concourse. In winter, there is an enticing small ice rink in the courtyard, and at Christmas time the lanes are always sensationally decorated.

There are two wonderful toy stores in the Bloor-Yorkville area. **The Toy Shop**, on Cumberland Street just east of Bay Street, has two floors of great stuff, including top-of-the-line toys. A bubble-blowing bear has stood guard at the entrance for as long as anyone can remember. The other must-shop is **Science City**, in the concourse under Holt Renfrew on Bloor Street. This store carries a superb selection of science-related

Toronto's kids' eats

Toronto has thousands of restaurants which serve just about every type of world cuisine, from Tibetan to Tex-Mex. If you are lucky enough to have kids who are adventurous eaters, you should try sampling some of the city's ethnic eateries, many of which are concentrated in the neighbourhoods described in this chapter. Most offer satisfying, interesting food at inexpensive prices and are casual enough that families with young children will feel welcome.

If, on the other hand, your kids look at any unfamiliar dish with suspicion, try one of the following eateries for a welcoming atmosphere and a kid-friendly menu.

Chuck E. Cheese's: Pizza and salad bar, but the real action is in the midway-style games for older kids and token-operated rides for the little ones. Sheer bedlam on weekends. Northeast suburban location at 2452 Sheppard Avenue East, 497-8855.

Druxy's Famous Deli Sandwiches: Numerous downtown locations, several in the downtown core's underground food courts, and at the Eaton Centre and the Royal Ontario Museum. Cafeteria-style service of deli meat sandwiches, plus other standbys like egg and tuna salad, hot dogs, and vegetable salads. Good spot to pick up fixings for a picnic.

Fran's Restaurants: Three locations open 24 hours, serving a wide range of mainstream dishes, a kids' menu, and Fran's Famous Pies, in a family-style setting.

Future Bakery: Four locations with cafeteria-style service and hearty eastern European fare — cabbage rolls, blintzes, borscht, schnitzels — along with excellent breads and cakes.

Ginsberg & Wong: Offers an interesting combination of Chinese and deli fare in a big and bright restaurant with an open kitchen. Huge portions at reasonable prices and a great kids' menu. Located in the Village by the Grange on McCaul Street, 979-3458.

Golden Griddle: Three downtown locations open 24 hours and serving pancakes, waffles, all-day breakfasts, and burgers.

Il Fornello: Nine locations serving "gourmet" pizza with a choice of scores of ingredients, plus pasta and some other Italian entrees, in slightly upscale surroundings. The kids' menu at $4.95 includes a soft drink and ice cream.

Lick's Burger & Ice Cream: Five locations serving great burgers, hot dogs, fries, and 30 or so ice cream specialties in a busy, casual setting, most with a kids' play corner.

Mars Food: Few things have changed in this unpretentious little place, established in 1951. Kids love sitting on stools along the Formica counter to watch the cooks at work. The menu boasts a huge selection, ranging from the classic all-day breakfast to steaks, salads, and Mars's famous muffins. Located at 432 College Street (at Bathurst Street), 921-6332. There's also a newly opened **Mars Uptown** at 2361 Yonge Street, 322-7111. Unlike the authentic downtown eatery, the uptown restaurant is retro-'40s style, complete with juke boxes, bright colours, and lots of chrome.

Mr. Greenjeans: A favourite Toronto family restaurant that features movie-poster-lined walls, hundreds of CDs hanging from the ceiling and an arcade with pool tables and video games. There's plenty to keep kids occupied as they devour large portions of the restaurant's specialties including burgers, fish, steak, chicken, and pasta. Kids' menu available. Located in the Eaton Centre, 979-1212.

The Organ Grinder: Pizza and pasta served in a cavernous downtown restaurant with video games and a restored Victorian pipe organ. 56 The Esplanade, 364-6517.

Swiss Chalet: Four downtown locations serving barbecued chicken and ribs in a family-style setting.

toys, books, and equipment that can't be matched anywhere else. Once they're let loose in here, your kids will have to be bribed to leave.

Places to eat in the Bloor-Yorkville area are numerous and varied. Recommended for their appeal to kids are **Flo's**, 10 Bellair Street, for its '40s-diner retro atmosphere; **Mövenpick**, 133 Yorkville Avenue, for its fabulous desserts and attention to young children; **The Coffee Mill**, inside the courtyard at 99 Yorkville, for its casual continental menu, with great cakes and strudels and tall raspberry sodas; and **Parisco Café On-The-Park**, 120 Cumberland Street, for its scrumptious Belgian waffles and views over Yorkville Park.

Walk #5
The Danforth
(Greektown)

Where? Danforth Avenue between Broadview and Pape Avenues
Start: Danforth and Broadview
Finish: Withrow Park, off Carlaw Avenue one block south of Danforth
How long? 2 hours, with stopover in Withrow Park

A visit to the Danforth (as Bloor Street east of the Don Valley is called) has lots of family appeal, and first among the area's attractions is food. The ten-block strip between Broadview and Pape Avenues is renowned for its many Greek restaurants, most with colourful sidewalk patios and affordable menus. On week-end evenings in the summer, you'll see line-ups of families and young singles waiting for tables at their favourite *tavernas*, which are almost as crowded at midnight as they are at dinner time. But before we get down to eating, let's savour some of the Danforth's other offerings.

Start your Danforth stroll on the north side at the corner of Broadview and head a few doors east to **Daisy House Dollhouses and Miniatures**, at 128 Danforth. Youngsters will be entranced by the window display of minutely detailed Victorian reproduction and contemporary dollhouses. Inside, they'll be transported

**Walk #5 The Danforth
(Greektown)**

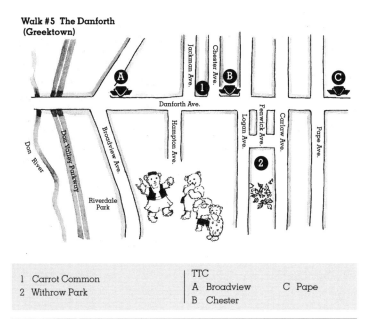

		TTC	
1	Carrot Common	A Broadview	C Pape
2	Withrow Park	B Chester	

into a miniature world, with microscopic washcloths for dollhouse loos and tiny plates of eggs and toast for the houses' little residents. The Daisy House has dollhouse kits for children and collectors, every sort of furniture and accessory, and building and finishing supplies for the do-it-yourselfer.

The heart of this stretch of the Danforth is indisputably the oddly named **Carrot Common**, a cluster of shops and restaurants built around a courtyard, at the corner of Jackman Avenue. This modest piazza is a gathering place for the stroller set, who congre-

gate here in droves on sunny days. The Common's designers have used a series of low-rise connected retail spaces, which extend back from the street to a small parking lot, to create a real town square and community meeting spot. One wonders why more architects don't follow their lead.

The common's shops are an eclectic mix of New Age and yuppie boutiques. The children's clothes at **Snug** and **Kidaroo** are practical and fashionable, and both shops carry some chic and comfortable outfits for moms too. **Gifts from the Earth** draws kids in with its window displays of

189

giant amethysts and sparkling blocks of quartz. This lapidary shop has hundreds of rocks and minerals on display, and is a real mecca for junior geologists. There are also books on crystals and other New Age healing techniques, jewellery, and nature-sounds audiotapes. Just east of the courtyard there is a **Book City** bookstore with a great magazine browser's rack at the front and a small kids' corner at the back. Between the **Postables** and **Pulp** shops you'll find everything you need in stationery and school supplies, gift wrappings, cards, and stickers.

The source of the name Carrot Common is a health-food supermarket, **The Big Carrot**, at the back of the mini-mall. The owners of this successful cooperative business are the developers behind the common — sort of small-scale New Age Reichmanns. The Big Carrot, one of the largest stores of its kind in Canada, is a place where you can choose from six types of tamari sauces or pick up a bundle of nutritious seaweed. At the rear of

The many people of Toronto

Toronto is said to be home to over 70 ethnic groups speaking over 100 languages, and it's gratifying to report that racial and ethnic harmony is the rule rather than the exception. Many groups have their own informally designated neighbourhoods, but a rich commingling does occur. For locals, one of the city's greatest appeals is to see Portuguese families browsing through the sari shops of Little India on Gerrard Street East, or Jamaican families tucking into bowls of steaming Vietnamese noodles in a Spadina Avenue restaurant.

Toronto's largest ethnic groups, in descending order of population size, are: British, Italian, Chinese, Portuguese, Jewish, East Indian, German, French, Greek, Polish, Ukrainian, Dutch, Spanish, Korean, Filipino, and Japanese.

the store is a deli take-out counter with a few tables. The daily soup is always delicious and the servers will make up a plateful of tasty salads from the 20 or so available. This is where good-for-you meets tastes-good, although some kids might find the ingredients a little too exotic.

My sons claim that **Sanelli's Cookery** in the common makes the best pizza in the world, probably because they started gumming it when they were still in diapers, and with the exception of that little place in Sorrento (or was it Naples?) I'd have to agree. Afterwards, you can choose between **The Fresh Pot** and **Just Desserts** — its spotted-cow upholstery is a big hit with kids — for cake and cappuccino.

On the south side of Danforth, just west of the Carrot Common, **Another Story** bookstore, at no. 261, specializes in kids' books and books on women's and third world issues. There's a table and chairs where the kids can read while you browse.

Treasure Island Toys, 311 Danforth, is a high-quality toy shop with friendly, helpful staff who try hard to answer those "What should I get for a ..." questions that come up at Christmas and birthdays. There's always a table-top train set out for the little ones to play with.

Also on the south side, **Jovenia** clothing store at no. 395 has reasonably priced kids' clothes, with lots of mix-and-match plain leggings, sweatpants, turtlenecks, and sweatshirts in bright primary colours. Farther along, older kids will be intrigued by the large selection of comic books, new and vintage, at **Unknown Worlds**, 429 Danforth, which carries books, comics, and games with sci-fi, fantasy, horror, and occult themes. **It's My Party**, 573 Danforth, has every kind of party supply you'll ever need, including stuff for those ubiquitous loot bags. The store's eye-catching window displays feature scores of seasonally coloured, wildly blowing balloons that always draw a small crowd.

If the time of year is suited to picnicking, you can stock up on supplies — crusty rolls, take-out salads, meats, cheeses, and every kind of fruit that's in season — at **Sun Valley Fruit and Grocery**, 583 Danforth. Then head south on Carlaw Avenue one block to **Withrow Park**, one of the city's loveliest neighbourhood parks. The park has a great "tot lot" — a fenced playground for younger kids with a wading pool and lots of play equipment — and another open playground for older children. There is also a playing field, skating rink, tennis courts, toboggan hills, picnic tables, a baseball diamond, and washrooms, not to mention the glorious stands of mature trees, which invite you to spread a blanket and just sit and watch the local residents tossing balls and walking their dogs.

For those not dining al fresco, the Danforth's selection of family-friendly restaurants is almost inexhaustible. If souvlaki and other Greek fare appeal, head for **Omonia Restaurant and Tavern** at 426 Danforth; the slow-turning spits of roast pig and gyros in the front window signal the authentic Hellenic fare within, and the efficient professionalism of the servers is welcome to families who don't want to linger. A meal here, or in most of the other modest Greek eateries on the strip, ranges between $4.95 for a souvlaki on a bun with some garlicky tzatziki to $9.95 for grilled lamb chops, with the usual Greek sides of both rice and potatoes, and a feta-sprinkled salad.

If you fancy more of a selection and a somewhat more upscale Mediterranean decor, try **Pappas Grill**, 440 Danforth, a bustling three-level restaurant that offers all the usual Greek specialties, plus pasta, pizza cooked in a wood-burning oven, burgers and various meat and fish entrees. Its two-tier display of cakes and pies delights with seemingly endless choices. A meal for a family of four, with wine, can be had here for about $80. **Ouzeri**, at 500A Danforth, serves a daily *mezes* lunch — a kind of Greek *dim sum* in which dozens of small dishes are brought to the table for patrons to pick and choose. At the end of the meal, the empty plates and bowls are totted up to arrive at the tab. Because the servings are small, and the choice is great, there's a good chance that everyone in your family will find something to his or her taste. At night, Ouzeri has a feature that most kids find irresistible: for a few dollars they'll provide you with a small stack of dishes for smashing, in high-spirited *taverna* tradition! If you want to take home some Greek treats, check out the cheese and spinach pies at **Athens Pastries**, 509 Danforth, or the dessert pastries at **7 Stars Bakery**, 544 Danforth.

Walk #6 Queen Street West Village

Where? Queen Street, west of University Avenue
Start: Queen Street West and University Avenue
Finish: Queen Street West and Spadina Avenue
How long? 2 hours

The stretch of Queen Street West between University Avenue and Bathurst Street is home to Toronto's thriving avant-garde art community. People dressed in black with rings through unexpected parts of their anatomy, vintage clothing stores, tattoo parlours, trendy eateries, and unique bookstores make the Queen Street West Village a popular strip for strolling. You can easily mix your excursion to Queen West with a trip to either the **Art Gallery of Ontario** or **City Hall** and the **Eaton Centre**, if you're inclined to make a day of it.

If you start at Queen Street

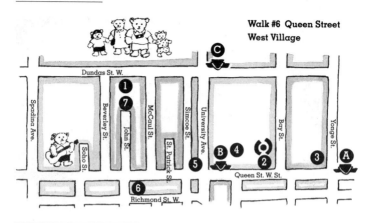

Walk #6 Queen Street West Village

1 Art Gallery of Ontario	7 Grange Park	
2 City Hall		
3 Eaton Centre	**TTC**	
4 Osgoode Hall	A Queen	
5 Campbell House	B Osgoode	
6 Citytv/MuchMusic	C St. Patrick	

and University Avenue, you can pop into either **Osgoode Hall** (see page 168) or **Campbell House** (see page 169) for a little legal lore. As you head west, you'll come upon **Dragon Lady Comics**, 200 Queen West, and **The Silver Snail**, 367 Queen West, which specialize in comic books — new and old — and related merchandise. **Bakka Book Store**, at no. 282, is Toronto's science fiction bookstore with a huge range of paperbacks, hardcovers, and magazines, and an impressively knowledgeable sales staff. The other two big bookstores on Queen West are **Edwards Books & Art** at no. 356,

which has a children's section and some discounted kids' titles, along with an extensive selection of art and lifestyle titles, and **Pages Books & Magazines**, at no. 256, which has only a modest children's section, but is a first-rate spot for adult browsing.

Liberated parents might want to point out the **Condom Shack**, at no. 231, to their off-spring: here's an opportunity for some on-the-spot sex education with a novel twist. Nearby at 299 Queen West is the **Citytv/MuchMusic** building, with its ornate Venetian-style facade. This is the head-quarters of media cool, and you might see a rock celebrity or two through the street-level studio windows. At the west end, you can drop a loonie into the Speaker's Corner box and let the kids state their views on whatever fires them up: if Citytv likes what your children have to say, they'll be shown on air. At the east end of the building, don't miss the Citytv car bursting out from the wall with its wheels spinning. On weekdays Citytv offers a free tour package that includes being part of the studio audience for a live broadcast of the "Lunch Television" program from 11:30 am to 12:30 pm, followed by a one-hour tour of the studios. For those who want to visit only the studio, tours depart at 2 pm. To make the necessary advance bookings for these tours, or to participate in the audience of "Lunch Television" or the popular "Cityline" show (10 am, Mondays to Fridays), call 591-5757.

Zephyr, at 292 Queen West, is a treasure trove with an eclectic mix of great gifts and toys. There are framed exotic insects and butterflies, unusual instruments, shells, beads, beautifully finished sculpture rocking toys, mobiles, and puzzles. Zephyr is a promising source for hard-to-buy children's presents. **Grafix** at

344 Queen West has every sort of art supply you might ever need, and at very competitive prices. Most kids love to cruise the shelves here, looking at all the different paints, markers, crayons, paper supplies, and art-related gizmos; they'll find anything they need to put together a school project. **The Games Workshop**, 331 Queen West, specializes in high-end war games sets; there's a playing area in the middle of the store and a table where kids can sit down to paint the small figures that come with each fantasy set.

There's an abundance of great eating spots on Queen West, from the haute-trendy to Harvey's hamburgers. It's never too soon to introduce young gourmets to the pleasures of a French kitchen at **Le Sélect Bistro** at no. 328 Queen West. This restaurant, which serves prix-fixe three-course dinners for $16, has a cozy atmosphere with bread baskets suspended from the ceiling and a lovely skylit backroom with banquettes. They serve a kids' menu at half the à la carte price. **Peter Pan**, at no. 373, was the first restaurant to open when the Queen West area began its renaissance in the '70s, and it's still a reliable choice with an appealing post-war diner decor. Eclecticism reigns at **The Bamboo**, 312 Queen West, which is also a nightclub. It's open for lunch on Saturdays and families find its relaxed ambiance congenial, with enough variety on the menu — from Thai noodles to hamburgers — to satisfy most tastes. There's also a couple of pinball machines to provide a distraction when young natives get restless.

If you're in the mood to picnic, head for the **Queen Street Market**, at no. 238, housed in a charming building that was originally occupied by a poultry wholesaler. Here you'll find all the fixings for a meal which you can eat in the small square behind the market. There's a deli selling meat and cheese, a bakery with big crusty buns, a shop with pizza slices and Italian sandwiches, a vegetarian take-away counter, and a greengrocer's. Or try the wholesome fare at **Earthtones**, a vegetarian cafeteria at no. 357 that also sells many flavours of frozen yogurt.

West of Spadina, attractions become a little spottier, but

there are still lots of interesting small shops to poke around in. If you make it all the way over to Bathurst Street, head a bit farther west and reward yourselves with a pit stop at the **Future Bakery** (739 Queen West), a hip and casual licensed café that serves a hearty east European menu and great baked goods. It's noisy and hectic and kids fit right into the general hubbub.

Other great neighbour-hoods

In addition to these walking tours, don't hesitate to explore some of the city's other distinctive neighbourhoods and to sample the sights,

sounds, smells, and tastes of the following vibrant communities.

Chinatown

Several blocks surrounding the intersection of Dundas Street and Spadina Avenue

Toronto actually has several Chinese-dominated neighbourhoods, but this one is still the largest and the busiest. On a weekend you'll find it tough slogging just to make it through the crowds that throng the sidewalks shopping for exotic-looking vegetables and other specialties. It's as if the stores themselves are just an adjunct to the main place of business. If you're in search of any kind of Chinese restaurant — Hunan, Szechuan,

Cantonese, Mandarin — or Vietnamese cuisine, you'll not be disappointed.

Kensington Market
West of Spadina Avenue, north of Dundas Street

Nowhere is Toronto's mosaic of ethnic groups more evident than in "the Market," as the area is often called. In earlier years, new immigrants to the city first settled here, before gradually moving on to more prosperous neighbourhoods. Today you'll find shops catering to just about every nationality: on a recent visit I noted stores run by Somalis, Ethiopians, Koreans, Jamaicans, Portuguese, Italians, Sri Lankans, and Thais — and that's only a random sampling.

Little India
Gerrard Street west of Coxwell Avenue

The delicious aromas of curry and exotic spices greet you as soon as you enter this colourful stretch of Gerrard Street East. Home to Toronto's large South Asian community — Indians, Pakistanis, Sri Lankans — Little India boasts numerous restaurants that offer some of the tastiest and cheapest food in the city along with sari shops and grocers that cater to the needs of the local clientele.

Little Italy
College Street west of Clinton Street

You'll know you're in the right place when you see the outline

of the map of Italy on the lamp standards along this lively stretch of College Street. In recent years, this neighbourhood has evolved into a destination for lovers of fine Mediterranean cuisine served in casually chic eateries.

Mirvish Village and Bloor Street West

Bloor Street west of Spadina Avenue to Markham Street

This stretch of Bloor Street is part of what is known as the Annex, a neighbourhood that has been home to generations of students from the nearby University of Toronto. A stroll along any of the leafy streets that run north from Bloor Street will give you a chance to admire the neighbourhood's stately Victorian homes, many of which have been converted to student accommodations. The area has a counter-culture feel blended with a highly diverse ethnic mix, and it is the best place in the city to find Hungarian food. **Mirvish Village** on Markham Street houses a lively mélange of shops and restaurants in a block of brightly painted Victorian houses. Bargain hunters will be drawn to the challenge of **Honest Ed's**, Ed Mirvish's landmark cut-rate emporium at the corner of Bloor and Bathurst.

10: The year at a glance

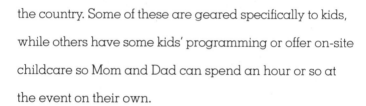

Toronto plays host to dozens of annual events, shows, and commercial expositions that draw visitors from around the province and across the country. Some of these are geared specifically to kids, while others have some kids' programming or offer on-site childcare so Mom and Dad can spend an hour or so at the event on their own.

The following listings are based on the most recent information available at publication. If you want to plan your time in Toronto to coincide with one of these events, call the number given to confirm the scheduling of the event and any other details that are important to you.

The dollar signs (**$$**) denote paid admission; **FREE** events are noted.

January

Mid-January: **Toronto Inter-national Boat Show** **$$**
Exhibition Place
591-6672

A huge expo of every type of watercraft from the smallest dinghy to luxury yachts, plus all the latest accessories. Features a Jet Age watercraft show with waterbikes, jet-skis, and other hydro vehicles; learn-to-sail and windsurfing simulators, a kids' fly-casting

contest, boating show, and swimwear fashions show.

Last Sunday: **Groundhog Winter Carnival   FREE**
Kortright Centre for Conservation
905-832-2289

Lots of outdoor fun and games, including "land ski" races, snow-snake games, falconry demonstrations, craft activities, cross-country ski trails, and guided nature walks.

February

Second weekend: **North York Winter Carnival   FREE**
Mel Lastman Square,
North York City Hall,
5100 Yonge Street
395-7350

An ice show spectacular with international skating stars. Non-stop entertainment performed at four stages. Fantasy snow playground, ice sculptures, and full midway, plus indoor kids' activities and pancake breakfasts. Most events are free.

Mid-February: **Canadian International Autoshow $$**
Metro Convention Centre,
255 Front Street West
905-940-2800

A ten-day expo of the latest model cars and other vehicles, plus all sorts of related accessories; 150 exhibitors. Daily kids' entertainment, 4x4 test track, mini speedway, slot-car racing.

201

Last weekend: **Annual Toronto Festival of Storytelling**
Harbourfront
924-8625
Celebrates the power of the spoken word and the cultural importance of stories, with tellers and tales from many traditions, plus music and dance. Includes special children's storytimes and concerts. Most family events are free.

March

First weekend: **Toronto International Bicycle Show** $$
Exhibition Place
363-1292
All the latest in bikes and biking gear, plus indoor mountain bike races, freestyle demos, and vintage bicycle displays.

First weekend: **National Hobby and Craft Show** $$
Exhibition Place
363-7442

An annual expo of the latest and most popular craft and hobby activities, with slot-car tracks, carpet races, childcare area with simple crafts, model railways, robotics displays, and the latest in kiddie craft sets.

Mid-March: **Zoom! International Children's Film Festival** $$
Harbourfront
973-4600
March Break screenings of the best in children's film and animation from around the world. Dozens of films, plus workshops on the latest in such technical film-making wizardry as computer animation.

Mid-March: **Toronto Sportsmen's Show** $$
Exhibition Place
695-0381
Canada's largest outdoors show lasts ten days and offers

kids' entertainment, Wild West rodeo show, retriever trials, pet shows, kids' trout pond, and Ontario Sports Centre with 20 activities.

April

Easter: Several events at various locations, including City Hall, Black Creek Pioneer Village, and many of the city's historic houses.

Last weekend: **One of a Kind Springtime Canadian Craft Show & Sale $$**
Exhibition Place
960-3680
Enjoy two floors of exhibits by craftspersons from across Canada. Lots of high-quality, handcrafted toys and kids' clothing; childcare area on site.

May

Victoria Day weekend:
Milk International Children's Festival $$
Harbourfront
973-4600
An annual first-rate theatrical event for families. Artists from over 15 countries stage over 100 performances of dance, puppetry, theatre, music, film, and storytelling.

Victoria Day (Monday):
Watch the **Queen's Birthday Parade** downtown; then in the evening, don't miss the **fireworks displays** at several city parks (**FREE**). Special Victoria Day events also happen at Black Creek Pioneer Village and other historic sites.

June

Mid-June: Metro International
Caravan **$$**
977-0466

For nine days, 40 community-sponsored pavilions throughout Metro host visitors for displays of ethnic art, food, and entertainment. Lots of join-in dancing and singing for all ages.

Last weekend: Toronto
International Dragon
Boat Race Festival   FREE
Toronto Islands
364-0046

Seventy teams race colourful 22-person Chinese dragon boats in the Centre Island lagoon. Cultural performances and displays of Chinese crafts and foods.

July

July 1: Canada Day
Celebrations   FREE
Nathan Phillips Square,
City Hall; Ontario Place;
Harbourfront

Daytime and evening concerts by top Canadian performers; large fireworks displays.

July 1: CHIN International
Picnic   FREE
Exhibition Place
593-9991

Sponsored by a multicultural radio and TV broadcasting company, this 400,000-person shindig has been dubbed the "largest outdoor free picnic in the world." Big-name performers from a variety of cultures appear; other attractions include lots of contests, games, displays, and food.

Second weekend: **Toronto Outdoor Art Exhibition FREE**
Nathan Phillips Square,
City Hall
408-2754

Hundreds of artists and craftspersons — local and from outside Metro — exhibit paintings, sculptures, glass, ceramics, jewellery, and other works.

Third weekend: **Molson Indy Toronto $$**
Exhibition Place
872-INDY

A three-day-long series of car races with a 280-kilometre (170-mile) race finale through blocked-off downtown streets and the CNE grounds.

Mid-July to August 1 weekend: **Caribana**
Free launch and wind-up concerts at Nathan Phillips Square; Music Festival on Toronto Islands ($$); plus several other events
925-5435

North America's largest street festival attracts one million

people in a celebration of West Indian culture. A spectacular, not-to-be-missed, eight-hour parade (**$$** for seated viewing at Exhibition Stadium) of 5000 revellers takes place on the second Saturday of the festival; for kids, there's also a Junior Carnival parade (**FREE**) on the first Saturday of the festival, which lets young participants show off their costumes.

August

Mid-August: Circle Ball Fair
FREE
Bloor-Yorkville
966-7880

An international festival of street performers with open-air acts by jugglers, theatre troupes, musicians, magicians, mimes, and more. Pavement artists create the world's longest art gallery along the Bloor Street sidewalk.

Mid-August to Labour Day:
Canadian National Exhibition **$$**
Exhibition Place
393-6000

Well into its second century, the start of the CNE signals the end of summer with a mind-boggling array of amusements and shows spread over the historic CNE grounds. Mondays are Kids' Days, with free admission for children 13 and under, and lots of special shows featuring kids' entertainers. On Tuesdays, everyone gets in free before noon. Daily attractions include the exuberantly tacky midway, a tamer kiddie midway for younger kids, the Human Adventure Area with even scarier thrills, virtual reality displays, free bandshell concerts, a petting zoo, animal exhibits, interactive sportsplay areas — and lots more. Be prepared to walk miles. Stroller rentals available, babysitting for ages three months to seven years at $1 per hour.

September

Last week: **Artsweek   FREE**
Various Venues
597-8223

Over 80 events showcasing the variety and vitality of Toronto's large arts community. The week features street parties with kids' entertainment at several sites, including the Young People's Theatre; open houses, tours, and performances. Most events are free.

Last Sunday: **Word On The Street   FREE**
Queen Street between University Avenue and Spadina Avenue
366-7421

This outdoor literacy fair turns Queen Street West into a publishers' bazaar. Displays by hundreds of book and magazine publishers, with contests and giveaways. KidStreet activities include entertainers, readings, plays, author and illustrator appearances.

October

Thanksgiving and Halloween:
Special events are scheduled at various sites, including Harbourfront, Black Creek Pioneer Village, Riverdale Farm, and Toronto Historical Board houses.

November

Second week: **Royal Agricultural Winter Fair $$**
Exhibition Place
393-6400

The world's largest indoor farm fair, the 11-day Royal is a must for kids with even the mildest interest in animals. Visitors can take in the sights, sounds, and

pungent smells of the Cattle Palace or the Horse Palace, stroll through a petting zoo, admire week-old pink piglets, stroke bunnies, and cock-a-doodle-do with roosters. There is special kids' entertainment, in addition to the numerous demos (butter sculpting is always popular), ongoing horse shows, and animal judging. Education Centres teach kids about farming and food-processing methods through displays, demos, and contests.

Second weekend: **The Parents (and Kids) Show $$**
Metro Convention Centre
869-0141

A three-day commercial expo of everything interesting to parents: toys, games, community services, fashions, food, health products, and computer software. There is a play area, kids' entertainment, and a free childcare area where the youngsters may be left while parents can take in seminars on childraising, nutrition, pregnancy, schooling, and medical issues.

Third Sunday: **Santa Claus Parade   FREE**
249-7833

A 90-year Toronto tradition, this is one of the world's most watched Christmas events, attracting 750,000 on-site viewers and untold millions on TV, in Canada and abroad. Two dozen animated floats, 1300 costumed children and marchers, and 20-plus bands make up the 6-kilometre (4-mile) parade, which starts on Bloor Street West and winds through Toronto's central core to Front Street.

Last week: **One of a Kind Christmas Craft Show and Sale $$**
Exhibition Place
960-3680

Canada's largest showcase of works by over 550 artisans. An excellent spot to buy original, high-quality toys and clothing for Christmas giving. Childcare area on site.

December

Mid-December: **National Ballet of Canada's** *The Nutcracker*   **$$**
O'Keefe Centre
393-7469

A holiday tradition not to be missed by young classical dance fans or their parents. The production is slated for a facelift in 1995, but you can be sure that the Sugar Plum Fairies, Snow Queen, and Bluebirds

Christmas events

Toronto celebrates the holiday season with festive displays, shows, and events all across the city. The following happenings are recommended for families.

WinterSong: Dances for a Sacred Season. The Canadian Children's Dance Theatre's holiday show offers spectacular dancing by young performers with choral accompaniment by the Toronto Children's Choir.

Christmas trees. Evergreens decorated in various folk traditions may be found at the Metropolitan Toronto Police Headquarters; designer-decorated trees at the George W. Gardiner Museum.

Victorian and Edwardian decorations. Recall earlier Toronto Christmases with decorations, games, and Yule treats at Toronto Historical Board houses.

Casa Loma's annual Christmas display. See themed decorations, Santa's Workshop, strolling storybook figures, and kids' entertainments.

Church of the Holy Trinity's Christmas pageant. The story of Christ's birth told with wondrous music, carols, and live tableaux.

Other seasonal activities: Throughout the Christmas school break, events take place at the Ontario Science Centre, Royal Ontario Museum, and Art Gallery of Ontario.

will be as magical as ever in this enchanting classic.

New Year's Eve: **First Night**   **$$**
Front Street between Jarvis and John Streets
362-8500

Coming up to its fifth anniversary in 1995, First Night has quickly established itself as a popular event with Toronto families in search of inexpensive, safe, and wholesome New Year's celebrations. For $7 First Nighters purchase a button that entitles them to attend as many as they wish of the festival's over 100 events, which include music and dance concerts, children's entertainments and activities, a People's Parade, and artworks.

Appendix 1
Help is a phone call away

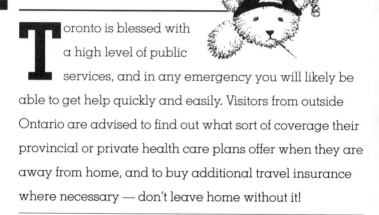

Toronto is blessed with a high level of public services, and in any emergency you will likely be able to get help quickly and easily. Visitors from outside Ontario are advised to find out what sort of coverage their provincial or private health care plans offer when they are away from home, and to buy additional travel insurance where necessary — don't leave home without it!

Emergency Ambulance, Fire and Police Services
Call 911
A 24-hour service. Your call will be directed to the appropriate agency.

Canadian Automobile Association (CAA) Emergency Road Service
222-5222
A 24-hour service for CAA and American Automobile Association members experiencing vehicle problems or in need of towing service.

Children's After Hours Clinics
235 Danforth Avenue
461-3000
1100 Sheppard Avenue East
250-5000
Drop-in medical clinics, staffed by pediatricians, operating outside normal office hours. Hours vary, but the clinics are generally open weekday evenings until 8:30 pm, and weekends and holidays from 10 am to 5:30 pm. Outside these hours, children exhibiting serious symptoms should be taken to the Hospital for Sick Children Emergency Department (see below) or to

any other hospital emergency department.

Dental Emergency Service
1650 Yonge Street
485-7121
Dental services offered seven days a week from 8 am to 12 am.

Distress Centres
598-1121
486-1456
A 24-hour telephone counselling service for those experiencing emotional distress.

Doctors Hospital Multilingual Health Service
45 Brunswick Avenue
923-5411
This hospital has a staff of interpreters and specializes in providing medical care to patients who wish to be served in languages other than English.

Hospital for Sick Children Emergency Department
555 University Avenue
813-1500 General switchboard
813-5900 Poison Control
Emergency Line
The best place to take children who have suffered serious accidents or are experiencing alarming symptoms. If your child's situation is not a genuine emergency, other options are available, such as a home visit or an after-hours clinic consultation. The Sick Kids' Emergency Department is often very busy and your wait could be long if your child's condition is not considered serious.

Medical Information Line
813-5817
A 24-hour telephone service, operated by the Hospital for Sick Children, offering information and advice on childhood illnesses and symptoms, provided by registered nurses.

Medvisit Doctors' Housecall Service
631-3000
Doctors will make home/hotel visits between 8 am and midnight for patients who are too ill to visit the family doctor, or who need attention after regular office hours. Services are fully covered by the Ontario Health Insurance Plan.

Mother Risk Hotline

813-6780

A telephone service, provided by the Hospital for Sick Children, that operates weekdays during business hours to advise expectant and nursing mothers of the risks associated with exposure to drugs, chemicals, and radiation.

The Parenting Education Centre of Ontario

333 Sheppard Avenue, Suite 210

512-8135

The Parenting Education Centre is a non-profit organization dedicated to improving the quality of parenting training and to assisting families to meet the challenges of raising children. Although the centre does not operate an officially designated help-line, callers to the centre seeking on-the-spot assistance with family issues will be offered advice or referrals.

Poison Hotline

Hospital for Sick Children

813-5900

A 24-hour advice and assistance service, provided by the Hospital for Sick Children, that offers advice following accidental poisonings or suspected poisonings.

Shoppers Drug Mart

700 Bay Street

979-2424

Open 24-hours for pharmacy and health-care products.

Travellers Aid Society

See page 19 for a full description of the services offered by this charitable organization.

Veterinary Emergency Clinic

1180 Danforth Avenue

465-3501

Provides 24-hour emergency pet care.

Appendix 2
No-cost Toronto

Much of Toronto can be enjoyed for free. Exploring its mosaic of neighbourhoods, hiking and birdwatching along wooded ravines, listening to buskers' outdoor concerts, jogging and biking along the Martin Goodman Trail, gallery-hopping in Yorkville, sampling the Saturday-morning bustle of the St. Lawrence Market — all of these are no-cost diversions that, along with many other adventures, can be experienced without opening your wallet. Several of the city's top attractions are free to the public at certain hours on specific days. These and some other free sites, tours, and performances are listed below.

Great Attractions for Free

Art Gallery of Ontario: Free admission on Wednesday evenings after 5 pm; be sure to visit Hands On! Off The Wall activity centre for kids; see page 114.

Harbourfront: Weekends feature the Kaleidoscope hands-on craft centre and Sunday-afternoon concerts; many seasonal and special events throughout the year also offer free activities; see page 69.

Ontario Science Centre: Admission by donation Wednesdays after 4 pm; see page 79.

Ontario Place: Free access daily to many activities, including the Children's Playground, Nintendo and Lego Pods, and several outdoor shows. Open Victoria Day weekend through Labour Day only; see page 75.

Royal Ontario Museum: Free admission every Tuesday after

4:30 pm; see page 84.

Toronto City Hall: Mondays–Fridays 8 am–4:30 pm buildings are open to the public for self-guided tours; most Nathan Phillips Square events are free; see page 64.

Other Free Attractions

Allan Gardens greenhouse; see page 132.

Canada's Sports Hall of Fame; see page 113.

Enoch Turner Schoolhouse; see page 99.

Holocaust Educational and Memorial Centre; see page 102.

Metropolitan Toronto Police Museum; see page 105.

Ontario Legislature (Queen's Park); see page 107.

Riverdale Farm; see page 143.

Toronto's First Post Office; see page 111.

Free Tours

The following organizations offer tours.

Canadian Broadcasting Corporation Broadcast Centre; see page 170.

National Ballet School (tours run September through June, Wednesdays and Fridays); see page 129.

Citytv studios; see page 195.

R.C. Harris Filtration Plant; see page 181.

Toronto Stock Exchange (viewing and presentation); see page 175.

Toronto Field Naturalists' Club (walking tour); see page 32.

University of Toronto (walking tour); see page 32.

Royal Ontario Museum (ROMWalks); see page 32.

Free Performances

Roy Thomson Hall: From October to April on Fridays at noon in the RTH lobby, enjoy concerts performed by young musicians; see page 128.

The Children's Book Store: Weekend concerts, readings, and demonstrations; see page 131.

Appendix 3
Books about Toronto
for kids

One of the best ways to involve kids in the planning and excitement of a trip is to have them do some reading about their destination. Happily, there are dozens of books about Toronto or set in Toronto to engage the interest of young readers of all ages. Here is a select list of recommended titles, arranged in ascending order of their age-appeal: books designed for the youngest readers appear at the beginning of each section.

Picture books, ages 3 – 7

Teddy Rabbit by Kathy Stinson (Annick Press, 1988)
Young Tony fears his beloved stuffed rabbit won't be welcome at the Centre Island Teddy Bears' Picnic.

Merry-Go-Day by Sheree Fitch (Doubleday Canada, 1991)
This fast-paced, poetic romp captures all the thrills and delights of a day at "The Ex" (Canadian National Exhibition).

Jonathan Cleaned Up – Then He Heard a Sound by Robert Munsch (Annick Press, 1981)
When his home inexplicably becomes the last stop on Toronto's subway system, Jonathan marches off to City Hall to set things right.

A Big City ABC by Allan Moak (Tundra Books, 1984)
Brightly coloured, naïve-art illustrations take you on a wide-ranging tour of the Toronto that kids like best

Take Me Out to the Ballgame by Maryann Kovalski
(North Winds Press, 1992)
Sing along to this old favourite song as Grandma takes the kids
on an exciting trip to the SkyDome.

Who Goes to the Park? by Warabe Aska (Tundra Books, 1984)
Poems accompanied by highly imaginative and beautiful
paintings reveal what High Park means to those who go there
throughout the seasons.

The Zoe Series by Barbara Reid (HarperCollins, 1991)
Illustrations created with intricately sculpted Plasticene evoke the
warmth and pleasure of everyday family life in the city.

The Red Caterpillar on College Street by Afua Cooper (Sister
Vision Press, 1989)
This collection of inner-city poems highlights Toronto's ethnic
diversity and cultural richness.

The Green Harpy at the Corner Store by Rosemary Allison
(Kids Can Press, 1976)
Funny things happen when this mythological creature with a
mean streak visits a modern-day family in Greektown on the
Danforth.

Fiction, ages 5 – 10

The Sandwich by Ian Wallace (Kids Can Press, 1975)
What can Vincenzo do when his school friends laugh at his
strange "stinky meat" sandwiches?

My Name Is Not Odessa Yarker by Marian Engel
(Kids Can Press, 1977)
Geraldine doesn't get too excited when her younger brother
decides to change his name, but when he changes hers as well,
she simply must protest!

Theft of Gold by J. Robert Janes (Scholastic, 1980)
Four children solve the mystery of the disappearance of priceless
gold nuggets from the Royal Ontario Museum.

Letting Go by Mary Woodbury (Scholastic, 1992)
Sara loves spending the summer with her grandmother on
Centre Island, but this year she finds herself struggling to cope
with too many changes, too fast.

Who Is Bugs Potter? by Gordon Korman (Scholastic, 1980)
He's a wicked drummer. Everybody thinks he's great, but no one
really knows who he is except Adam Webb, and he's not about
to tell.

Scoop Jones by Katie Gillmor Ellis (Prentice-Hall Canada, 1989)
New to Toronto, T.J. Jones wants desperately to fit in, to be some-
body, but her plan to win the *Courier* Junior Columnist contest
just isn't working out.

The Firefighter by Bernice Thurman Hunter (Scholastic, 1991)
Terry craves excitement but gets more than he bargained for
when he runs away from home and ends up accused of arson!

The Lost Treasure of Casa Loma by Eric Wilson (Clarke Irwin, 1980)
When the millionaire owner of Casa Loma is kidnapped for a
ransom of priceless diamonds hidden somewhere in the castle,
Tom and Liz follow the clues in search of criminals and treasure.

Cabbagetown Gang by Mark Thurman (NC Press Limited, 1987)
Based on the author's own childhood in Toronto's first public hous-
ing project, this is the story of the Regent Five Blood Brothers, a
group of boys dedicated to comic books, mischief, and no snitching.

The Booky Series by Bernice Thurman Hunter (Scholastic, 1981-85)
This trilogy of heart-warming novels introduces readers to Booky
Thomson, a young girl growing up in Toronto during the Great

Depression, whose indomitable spirit helps everyone make it through difficult times.

Hawk and Stretch by Bernice Thurman Hunter (Scholastic, 1993)
Booky's brother, Billy, and his bodyguard-cum-friend, Danny "Hawk" Thunder, look for adventure in World War II Toronto.

The Kids of Degrassi Street by Kit Hood and Linda Schuyler (James Lorimer, 1990-92)
Based on the popular TV series, each book contains three stories following the further adventures of this familiar cast of characters.

Fiction, ages 10 and over

The Sky is Falling,
Looking at the Moon,
The Lights Go On Again,
All by Kit Pearson (Viking Kestrel, 1989, 1991, 1993)
Fearing Hitler's invasion of England, Norah's parents send her and her younger brother to live with a rich stranger in Toronto. This trilogy presents a touching and insightful account of children's feelings when they are suddenly separated by war from all that is comforting and familiar.

The Tinderbox,
The Quarter-Pie Window,
The Sign of the Scales,
All by Marianne Brandis (The Porcupine's Quill, 1982, 1985, 1990)
This series of historical novels set in Upper Canada in the 1830s chronicles the life of an orphaned 13-year-old girl as she struggles to understand difficult events and emotions.

Fire Ship by Marianne Brandis (The Porcupine's Quill, 1992)
A young Canadian boy plays an important role during the American attack on the town of York and learns that war is not an exciting game, but a terrible tragedy for both sides.

Harriet's Daughter by Marlene Nourbese Philip (Women's Press, 1988)

A young Afro-Canadian girl struggles with her father and with her own identity in contemporary Toronto.

A Darker Magic by Michael Bedard (Atheneum, 1987)

A scary and exciting story unfolds as evil magic from the past invades the present and culminates in a dramatic struggle to save a friend.

Redwork by Michael Bedard (Lester & Orpen Dennys, 1990)

Curious to find out what the mysterious Mr. Magnus is doing in the garage out back, Cass and his new friend, Maddy, find themselves drawn into the secret world of alchemy.

On My Own by Mitzi Dale (Groundwood Books, 1991)

Kim Taylor quits high school and moves to Toronto to become an actress, but the road to fame is rockier than she could ever have imagined.

Me and Luke by Audrey O'Hearn (Douglas & McIntyre, 1987)

His girlfriend wants to give up their baby for adoption, but Matt just can't do it. With no one to turn to for help, Matt resorts to desperate measures.

Non-fiction

Toronto by Wendy and Jack Murphy (Blackbirch Press, Inc., 1992)

Easy-to-read text and lively pictures give an overview of the geography, history, people, and special places of Toronto.

Casa Loma and the Man Who Built It by John Denison (Boston Mills Press, 1982)

This guided tour includes lots of pictures showing the castle as it was in Sir Henry Pellatt's day, and many interesting facts and anecdotes about this larger-than-life Torontonian and his lavish home.

Black Creek Pioneer Village by Nick and Helma Mika (Mika Publishing, 1988)
Pictures and text describe this extensive collection of 19th-century buildings and explain the roles played by the structures and their inhabitants in pre-Confederation society.

Karen Kain, Born to Dance by Meguido Zola (Grolier, 1983)
Young dance enthusiasts will enjoy this account of Karen Kain's childhood and training at the National Ballet School in Toronto, which led to her career as principal dancer of the National Ballet of Canada and one of the world's most acclaimed ballerinas.

"Passengers Must Not Ride on Fenders" by Mike Filey (Green Tree Publishing, 1974)
Text and pictures show how Toronto's streetcars, the "Red Rockets," have played an important part in the city's social history and development.

The Toronto Story by Claire Mackay (Annick Press, 1990)
Full of fascinating lore about important historical events and figures as well as details of the everyday lives of ordinary people, this book explains how today's Toronto came to be.

Little by Little by Jean Little (Viking Kestrel, 1987)
Born in Taiwan to Canadian parents, nearly blind from birth, the popular children's author describes her early years in Toronto.

The following books contain many bright and colourful photographs of Toronto's people, places, attractions, and architecture.
Toronto by Roger Boulton (McClelland & Stewart, 1990)

Toronto: The City of Neighbourhoods by Marjorie Harris. (Key Porter/McClelland & Stewart, 1984)

Colorful Toronto by Joe Fisher (Totem Books, 1984)

Toronto by Duncan McDougall (Whitecap Books, 1983)

Bibliography

Gibbs Carpenter, Donna.
Daytripper 2: 50 Trips In and Around Toronto.
Toronto: Stoddart–Boston Mills Press, 1992.

Gould, Allan.
Fodor's Toronto.
New York: Fodor's Travel Publications, 1992.

Katz, Elliot.
Great Country Walks Around Toronto, Third Edition.
Toronto: Great North Books, 1993.

Labreque, Sue.
52 Weekend Activities for the Toronto Adventurer.
Vancouver: Whitecap, 1990.

Lansky, Vicki.
Trouble-free Travel with Children: Helpful Hints for Parents on the Go.
Deephaven, MN: The Book Peddlers, 1991.

Mackay, Claire.
The Toronto Story.
Toronto: Annick Press, 1990.

Mackenzie, Margaret and Rod.
Toronto: The Ultimate Guide.
Vancouver/Toronto: Douglas & McIntyre, 1992.

Wood, Marilyn.
Frommer's Comprehensive Travel Guide: Toronto '93-'94.
New York: Prentice-Hall Travel, 1993.

Photo credits

Art Gallery of Ontario: 115, 117
Bata Shoe Museum: 95
Black Creek Pioneer Village: 96
City of Toronto, Records & Archives: 65, 78, 88, 133 (top),
    135,137,143,147,149,150,163,164,172,198, 203
Citytv: 195
Delta Chelsea Inn: 35, 46
Enoch Turner Schoolhouse:100
First Light: 199
Four Seasons Hotel: 47
Glen Grove Suites: 36
GO Transit: 22 (left)
Harbourfront: 72, 148
Hockey Hall of Fame: 113
Anne Holloway: 89, 202
Brian A. Kilgore: 204
Samuel Kolber: 182, 184
Kortright Centre: 141, 201
Legislative Assembly of Ontario: 108
Live Entertainment of Canada Inc.: 127 (Fiona Spalding-Smith, photographer)
McMichael Canadian Art Collection: 119
Metro Toronto Zoo: 73, 74
Metro Works, City of Toronto: 181
Metropolitan Toronto Convention & Visitors Association: 13, 67, 76, 93, 176, 197, 205
Metropolitan Toronto Police: 106
Metropolitan Toronto Reference Library: 21 (Ted Wickson, photographer), 183
Olde Town Toronto Tours Limited: 29
Ontario Heritage Foundation: 126
Ontario Science Centre: 79, 80
Paramount Canada's Wonderland: 82
Royal Agricultural Winter Fair: 207
Royal Ontario Museum: 84, 85
St. Lawrence Centre: 162 (Robert C. Ragsdale, photographer)
Toronto Blue Jays Baseball Club: 138
Toronto Historical Board: 101, 103, 104, 109
Toronto Transit Commission: 22 (right), 24, 25, 28, 55, 57, 63, 70, 87,
    128, 133 (bottom), 154, 168, 171
Trillium Terminal 3: 17 (top and bottom)
Victoria University, University of Toronto: 43
Westin Harbour Castle: 50
Wild Water Kingdom: 156
Young People's Theatre: 124

Index

223

225

Anne Holloway has travelled widely and frequently in North America, Europe and points beyond, including Sri Lanka and the Canary Islands. Now the mother of two young boys, her travels keep her closer to home in Toronto, where she works as a writer, editor, and researcher. *Toronto with Kids* is her first book.

Toronto with Kids was designed and typeset by James Ireland Design Inc. The type is Adobe Memphis, a geometric slab serif, created in 1929 by Rudolf Weiss.

This book is bound using the Otabind process, a highly durable binding with a free floating cover that allows the book to lie flat when opened.

Maps for chapter 9 and illustrations by Pat Stephens Greater Toronto Area and Downtown Toronto maps by John Sapsford, Berlin Studios